POPE JOHN XXIII

POPE JOHN XXIII

A Life of the New Pope

BY ANDREA LAZZARINI

HERDER AND HERDER

THIS ENGLISH TRANSLATION BY MICHAEL HATWELL
IS BASED ON THE ORIGINAL ITALIAN VERSION OF
"GIOVANNI XXIII, LA VITA DI ANGELO G. RONCALLI"
PUBLISHED BY CASA EDITRICE HERDER, ROMA, 1958

SECOND IMPRESSION PUBLISHED 1959 BY
HERDER AND HERDER, INC., 7 WEST 46th STREET,
NEW YORK 36, NEW YORK

THE FOLLOWING FOREIGN LANGUAGE EDITIONS
HAVE BEEN PUBLISHED OR ARE IN ACTIVE PREPARATION:
GERMAN EDITION: VERLAG HERDER, FREIBURG
SPANISH EDITION: EDITORIAL HERDER, BARCELONA
PORTUGUESE EDITION: EDITORA HERDER, SAO PAULO
JAPANESE EDITION: HERDER-AGENCY, TOKYO

WITH ECCLESIASTICAL APPROVAL

LIBRARY OF CONGRESS CATALOG CARD NUMBER: 59—8776
© 1959 BY HERDER & CO GMBH, FREIBURG
MADE AND PRINTED BY HERDER-DRUCK,
FREIBURG, WEST GERMANY

TABLE OF CONTENTS

1. An Ancient Land   1

2. The Indepedent Farmers   7

3. Born a Second Time   13

4. The Count-Bishop   19

5. From Learning to Action   28

6. The Apostle of Youth   42

7. The First Missions   47

8. In France   67

9. Venice and Rome   82

10. The First Broadcast   92

11. Epilogue   99

    Notes   107

    List of Important Dates   133

    Index   135

    List of Illustrations

    Illustrations

1
AN ANCIENT LAND

BERGAMO does not really belong to Lombardy. The map of Italy says it does, but that was compiled in a hurry by a few Piedmontese colonels and prefects, during a short period known as the reign of the House of Savoy. They merged and confused all the old independent states and dukedoms to arrive at the somewhat arbitrary divisions we find in modern Italy, with the result that people of one region are, for administrative purposes, grouped together with other people of entirely different stock.

Bergamo is altogether different from Lombardy proper, and its people have hardly anything in common with the people of Milan, the chief town of the region. So much is this the case, that when noisy parties of Milanese holiday-makers pass through Bergamo on their way to the Casino at San Pellegrino or to the snow-fields of the Alps, it is as if the town had been invaded by foreign tourists. There, under the leafy avenue of Sentierone, they pile out of their cars and go blustering into cafes and restaurants where, after a moment or two, the smiling Bergamese resume their interrupted conversations.

Some say that this diversity of character had its origin in five hundred years of easy-going Venetian rule, and a kind of limpid sweetness is certainly to be found in the Bergamese character. But then, Brescia, too, was under the Venetians, and the Brescians could hardly be more different from the Bergamese: the former are just as dogmatic and unbending as the latter are cordial and easy to get on with.

Nogara, an authority on the Etruscans, is of the opinion that the Bergamese bent for painting and music gives evidence of their extremely ancient origins. He maintains that they are descended from those Etruscans who had sought refuge in the foothills of the Alps. Indeed, some scholars say that even today there exists a similarity between Tyrolean inns and Tuscan eating-houses; according to them, "Tyrol" is an Etruscan word.

But where, if it comes to that, have the Etruscans not lived – or at least camped overnight? The headstone of some poor bearded soothsayer can be read even in a trim little garden at Klagenfurt. And that huge copper vase that has been discovered at Vix – surely that is from the hands of Etruscan craftsmen?

There is to be found in upper Bergamo, a kind of

medieval Acropolis for the noble families of the town, a resemblance to Lucca and other places in Tuscany, the land where the Etruscans were most deeply rooted. The likeness is evident in the proportions of the buildings, the layout of certain streets and the design of certain squares; only the air is different, for there rises up from the plain an almost impalpable mist which enriches the reflections of light in Spring and late Summer and makes Bergamo a painter's city. Even today, there are eighty or so artist inhabitants. They will never be well known, but they go on working quietly and unhurriedly, sure of a market for their pictures – a state of affairs which has not been experienced anywhere else in Italy for two or three hundred years – for Bergamo is not just the home of industrialists, wealthy lawyers and surgeons who want life-size portraits painted in oils, but also of businessmen and accountants, who think it as natural to buy a landscape or a still life as to get a new car or give jewelry to their wives. And in the local art gallery on Sundays, it is not uncommon to meet shopkeepers and workmen who have managed to save up just enough money to go there and buy a picture for their home.

One day, about ten years ago, a promising young architect known for his advanced ideas, was visited by a simple workman. The man's wife had just died and, instead of going to the local mason for one of his brown marble tombstones, as the average Italian workman would have done, he had come to ask the architect to design him a really fine memorial in modern style.

Indeed, enthusiasm for the unusual is not lacking in the Bergamese; for example, when Nullo wanted to help in the liberation of Poland, the largest of the little groups that joined him in his mad undertaking was from Bergamo. Their whims, however, are born of a generous impulse. This being so, it is understandable that the Bergamese, in their fear of other people's duplicity and lack of sympathy, sometimes appear to be, or actually are, suspicious folk, almost diffident about the idea of facing life among strangers under other skies. It must be confessed that he who carries his heart in his hand has to be certain that its recipient is worthy of the gift.

Even their dialect helps the Bergamese to defend themselves, for it is a difficult mixture of words from all ages; it bristles with almost barbaric roots and expressions. In their accent there is hardly any trace of that sobbing cadence which is used in Milan and which dates back to the time of St. Ambrose. Indeed it rather resembles a pant as though the Bergamese were constantly in a state of breathless anticipation; which brings us back to where we began, talking of the good humor of the Bergamese.

Their wit, examples of which can be found in their literature as far back as the sixteenth century, is certainly one aspect of their frankness.

So, to this ancient spot whose vine-covered hillsides have all the sweetness of the Tuscan hills, with here and there the little cypress groves reminiscent of the Etruscan countryside, there came, at the beginning of the sixteenth century, from the mountains around the neighbouring Imagna valley, one Martino Roncalli, called by everyone "Maitino". He decided to settle there, but, before he could do so, it was necessary to drain the boggy plain called Sotto il Monte (Under the Mountain) and to plant the land – here rich, there poor – with crops and vines, in spite of the malaria which was rife.

Later, Maitino's children and other members of the Roncalli family left their native valley, and settled in many different places, with differing fortunes, but they all seem to have come from the village of Roncaglia di Cepino in the Imagna valley. It was from this place that they took their name early in the fifteenth century.

From thence the Counts Roncalli of Montorio, of Foligno and Rovigo, the Roncalli-Perettis, the Roncalli-Frosios and the Roncalli-Parolinis take their names. Looking at the different branches of the family in Bergamo and elsewhere, one discovers priests and monks, painters and physicians. The painter Pomarancio, for example, traces of whose considerable artistic production are still to be found in Rome, even in St. Peter's, was one Cristoforo Roncalli, called in accordance with a former usage, by the name of the Tuscan village where he had been born.

2

THE INDEPENDENT FARMERS

THIS Maitino began to drain the land, knowing that he was not losing the liberty he had enjoyed as a highlander. He was not a peasant, a serf in complete bondage to some count, but a tenant-farmer having the right to half the product of his own labor. The still boggy country belonged to a wealthy Bergamese, who lived in Bergamo itself on account of his trading activities, and only occasionally rode out to talk business with his tenant. While Maitino's contribution was the sweat of his brow, the landlord put his money into the farm – in a sense an equitable arrangement; and they agreed to halve the produce.[1]

Later Maitino acquired a piece of land on the slopes of Giovanni, where the first parish church of Sotto il Monte stood, and built, about the middle of the sixteenth century, a house whose outer walls facing the plain he had decorated by an itinerant artist with pictures of saints, which can still be seen today. They show the Madonna and Child, the holy Abbot Anthony, and Bernardine of Siena, favorite saints of those times. He also added the first Roncalli coat of arms, which contains the same battlemented tower to be seen in the coat of arms of the present Pope.

For more than a century and a half descendants of that first Maitino lived in their hillside dwelling. Then the family split up, some of them remaining in Sotto il Monte, the rest spreading throughout the district of Bergamo and beyond, taking other names.

At the beginning of the seventeenth century Maitino's last descendant, the priest Don Bernardo Roncalli, was living in the old house. After him it passed into the hands of other owners, among whom were the De Vecchis, Macassolis, Mangilis, and the Scottis. Today it belongs to the Scotti family from whom the present Pope has rented it ever since his consecration as bishop in 1925.

The Pope's immediate ancestors have always lived in Sotto il Monte, and it was here, on November 25, 1881, in a part of the town called Brusico, that he was born, the newest member of a large family which had been farmers for generations. The father, Giovanni Battista, was presented by his wife, Mariana (*née* Mazzola), with ten fine children. Angelo Giuseppi was the eldest boy. He was baptized by the parish priest, Don Francesco Rebuzzini, late the same evening.[2]

The sun governed the hard day's activities here, just as it does in country districts everywhere else, and so did the bell from the little Franciscan monastery on the hill, overlooking the vineyards, the orchards and the fields. When the monks rang it at noon, Angelo's mother usually remarked to her large flock of children: "Time to put the pot on." One description of their domestic life in those far-off days recalls that "there was never any meat at the family table, nor wine, nor dessert. In the morning, we had porridge; at noon, some vegetable soup and a little cheese or sausage, and the same again in the evening. We were very poor, but we were happy, and we were never aware that we lacked anything. In fact, we lacked nothing at all."

And yet there were so many of them to share those hard-won meals. Children were born, grew up and brought home from some nearby farm the wives they had chosen; and then grandchildren appeared. Holidays saw gathered at the farm the families of three brothers, with eighteen children between them. The Roncalli family now numbers thirty-five.[3] The happy father doubtless expected his eldest son would become a farmer like himself, but the ways of Providence were quite different from any which he in his modesty and goodness might ever have suspected. From Angelo's early childhood there was never any doubt that he would become a priest, and even at school his comrades were soon calling him respectfully, "Angelino, the little priest".

At Brusico, not very far from Sotto il Monte, old Battistel keeps his ironmonger's shop to this day. He is eighty now, but he can still remember the days he spent in the village school, the three classes all in the same classroom, and Donizetti, the teacher, walking up and down, trying to cope with them all at once. Battistel was in the top class – he was having to pass through it a second time, as he hadn't done very well the previous year – and he used to sit at the very back of the room. In the front desk, where they put the clever ones, sat young Angelo. Battistel says, "Angelo Roncalli always grasped everything at once. He was only in the bottom class, but he was far and away cleverer than any of us in the top class, and we felt even in those days that he was sure to become famous."

His younger brother Giuseppe says more or less the same thing. "Ah, but Angelo's a sharp one. He never forgets a face, even if he's only seen it once before. He may have first noticed it, as a young priest, in the middle of a congregation, but he'll still remember it now. He's been like that ever since he was little."

So clever was he in fact, that when he had finished at the village school his parents took the – for them – enormous decision to send him to a secondary school.

Meanwhile, the parish priest, a saintly man, had begun to read the psalms with the boy, who enjoyed reciting them with him. Soon afterwards he sent him to Don Pietro Nolis, the young parish priest of nearby Carvico, in order that he might give him a start in Latin. He was a successful pupil and at the age of eight or nine entered the beautiful diocesan college in Celana, which lies between Pontida and Somasca, where he started as a day-boy. These were difficult days indeed, for whilst the little town of Celana is not, as the crow flies, so very far away from the family home, the road was not good, and it took Angelo two hours to walk each way. He never got home until after dark, then he had to have something to eat and begin reading his lessons by candlelight. It was too much for him. As a result of the lessons, the homework and the journey, it was not long before he became ill. The fair hopes of his village school days under Donizetti had seemingly come to nothing, and he became more and more discouraged as he tried to beguile the dreary, heartbreaking walk into Celana by throwing stones into the hedges that bordered the road.

His parents decided that it was a waste of time for him

11

to continue and made up their minds to ask a local priest to persuade him to give up his hopes for the future. They wrote a letter and gave it to Angelo to deliver, but sensing that there was something amiss, he stopped on the way, opened the letter, read it – and tore it up. This story is vouched for, but it is impossible to discover the outcome; it serves, however, to show how near he came to giving up and going out to work on the farm like the rest of the family.

Angelo quickly surmounted his temporary antipathy towards learning. He was obviously made for the priesthood, and was indeed accepted at the diocesan junior seminary of Bergamo in November, 1892, at the age of ten; moving up, at the age of fourteen, into the major seminary.

On the eve of his departure, his mother tried to scrape together a little money for him. The rector had told her that her son would have to take some with him, and had advised her to make a collection round the family. Assunta Marchesi, the Pope's sister, tells us that her mother left home that morning and didn't return until evening. She walked in, laid two lira on the table, (very roughly equal to three dollars today) and broke into loud sobs.

3

BORN A SECOND TIME

THE child in the seminary is created anew, heart and mind. Not only has the spirit to be moulded, but the flesh itself must be transmuted into the consecrated flesh of the Catholic priest. So in the ancient seminary of Bergamo Angelo Roncalli was gradually reborn, drawing from thence that blood, that living spirit, which in those days the Church herself felt to be pulsing in her veins. If he had been prepared in a seminary other than that of his own diocese, he would have emerged as a priest of quite different character, just as would have been the case had his initiation taken place ten or fifteen years earlier. He emerged, however, in 1902, the special product of the Guindani[1] administration, under which Bergamo had begun to establish itself as an example of what all Italy would become once the Catholics had reconquered it, inch by inch.

Today, after so many social and political changes have taken place, bringing with them improvements in the public life of Italian Catholics, it is easy to take a detached view of their reconquest of Italy. But holding out, day by day, during those difficult years, was a hard, sometimes heroic, struggle. And yet not only leading Catholics took part in it, but also a great many simple folk deliberately risked loss of livelihood and contentment. Sometimes they offered with quiet shy humility the sacrifice of an oppress-ed, tortured existence, in the naive faith that all the hills of Rome, except the Quirinal, had been reconquered.

However it may be, whether leading or led, all of them avowed their Catholicism openly, freely and actively. They rebuilt their native land in the consciences of its citizens and in laws worked out according to the tradi-tional patterns of its culture. They fought and suffered. And the first among them, it can be said today without flattery, were the Bergamese.

Throughout the rest of Italy people were asking themselves: "If Catholics have achieved so much in Bergamo, perhaps it would be worth our while to follow their example." There were forty-five thousand organized Catholics in the diocese, ranging from students to work-men. With a network of seventy-seven parish councils, orders from the bishop could reach even the most distant mountain parishes reliably and quickly; and back along the same channels from every parish, every hamlet, every farm, there daily flowed information about the economic, political and social life of the area.

The young people who had discovered themselves growing up, living and working under an anti-Catholic regime, had formed themselves into forty young people's circles, of which the pioneer group came into being as early as 1868.

For the lower classes, crushed by the economic *laissez-faire* and ignored by those in power, there were mutual aid societies for all, a people's bureau, workmen's clubs, from sixty to seventy agricultural aid groups, forty-five co-operative animal husbandry centers, communal kitchens, farmer's associations, a diocesan bakery, a co-operative dairy and, last of all, a bank.

To assist in the formation of the clergy as a responsible class of leaders there were the thirty members of the Ecclesiastical Union for Social Studies, who were active during Roncalli's last few years as a student, at a time when he began to look at the world with his own eyes and to sum it up for himself. And at the bishop's side, there were to be found, as his cleverest and most faithful helpers, not priests, as one would have expected, but two laymen, Count Medolago and Niccolò Rezzara.[5] So Don Roncalli formed, out of his youthful experience at Bergamo, that conception of the Church as the collaboration of

15

priests and laity, which he was to keep for the rest of his life.

The adolescent seminarian had now to undergo a second rebirth which would bring him nearer to perfection. After Bergamo had done its initial work, it was the turn of Rome to remould his character. From the raw Bergamese priest still had to emerge the polished Roman. His transfer to the capital was actually a reward, for only the most intelligent seminarians are sent there to complete their studies and to take degrees.[6] It is these priests who are destined to be the future administrators of the Church. She is not concerned whether a priest is the son of a prince or a wine-grower, as was Angelo Roncalli, but she does insist that the posts of command be entrusted to men who, from their youth, have developed in the shadow of the Vatican. That is why, in the Vatican, negro students, brought up, perhaps, in the jungle, can be found rubbing shoulders with young priests from America who find it impossible to adandon the habit of baseball between lectures. In the end they all become Romans.

It is sufficient here to say that there is one kind of "Roman-ness" which has practically nothing in common with the erudition of those who spend their time in the libraries, among the archives, or exploring the archaeological excavations. Perhaps it is more the legendary character of the Romans, which so annoys foreigners at first, but which, given a little time, can finally bewitch and teach them how to get the most out of life. This quality is something magnanimous; it springs from a real knowledge of life, and of human experience gained by dint of walking day after day through the narrow alleys where ancient buildings now provide homes for the people. At the same time as he is assimilating this Roman spirit, the seminarian must re-form his temperament and his character, not to mention his soul. Perhaps the English, with their public school tradition, will be best able to understand the radical importance which the years spent between the basilicas and the libraries of Rome have in the formation of a priest.

Throughout the Catholic world, already so vast and yet ever increasing, there is a fundamental unity of faith and discipline. This unity had a value for everyone, especially the clergy, but among this particular group that has studied in Rome and whose members range from venerable cardinals to young seminarians, there is to be found a greater affinity, a closer harmony, and a more complete unity, which, we suggest, derives from that intuitive and friendly, realistic, traditional, generous — in fact, altogether human, Roman spirit.

The journey to Rome was naturally a propitious one for

Angelo Roncalli, especially as it took place during the Holy Year of 1900. The young man found himself not simply in the Eternal City, but there during a period – and a long one too – when the Church was more than ever alive and universal, a fact that even her adversaries were unable to deny.

Leo XIII composed a Latin hymn to the new century, perhaps the only tribute which was not the vehicle for magniloquent and naively hopeful faith in progress. For it believed in progress, this new century, with its streams upon streams of people from all nations and with its representative committees and organizations which had been set up in every country with a view to eliminating the State.

4

THE COUNT-BISHOP

ANGELO Roncalli was ordained on August 10, 1904, by Monsignor Ceppetelli, in the Church of Santa Maria in Monte Santa, Rome, one of the twin churches that stand on opposite corners at the end of the Corso where it enters the Piazza del Popolo.

On the following day he offered his first Mass in St. Peter's, at the altar of the Confession which is situated immediately above the tomb of the Apostle. He then travelled to Sotto il Monte to say his second Mass there, and one of the people present still remembers the village doctor jokingly suggesting that Don Roncalli would become Pope.

Scarcely six months later, on January 29, 1905, a famous priest, not young but still very vigorous, was consecrated bishop in the Sistine Chapel. He was Monsignor Giacomo Radini-Tedeschi, and the ceremony marked the end of his Vatican career. He was being sent from Rome to take over the see of Bergamo. It was Pope St. Pius X's particular wish that he should go there, instead of to a quiet and restful diocese, or even archdiocese – for both Palermo and Ravenna had been suggested to him as possible sees for Radini-Tedeschi. The Pope had replied, however, that a bishop should never be content with anything less than the most important diocese in Italy.

The new bishop, whose father, Count Carlo Radini-Tedeschi, had fought so energetically to protect ancient legacies left in charity to the poor from the machinations of the lawyers, was one of the front line fighters in the struggles between Church and State in Italy at that time. By his appointment he was being entrusted with the responsibility for the whole Italian Catholic revival.[7]

That St. Pius X laid great stress on Radini-Tedeschi's preferment, may be deduced from the fact that the Pope himself consecrated him in the Vatican. The ceremony was followed by a reception, held in the famous Borgia Suite, and in the evening a gala dinner took place in the Consistory Hall. As a farewell commendation, the Pope issued a Brief confirming him in charge of the pilgrimages to Lourdes and the Holy Land.[8] In addition the future saint promised the new bishop that as soon as he was dead he would come and take him, and that they would remain together eternally. This promise disturbed the young prelate at the time, and although he never forgot it, it was not until he was in fact dying that he realized its

full significance. The present Pope, to whom Radini-
Tedeschi confided this matter only when on the point
of death, tells us about it in the moving pages which
speak of the bishop's quiet and peaceful passing.[9]

After his consecration Radini-Tedeschi learnt that two
of the young priests and seminarians who had assisted at
the altar were from Bergamo. He was advised to
appoint one of them as his secretary and chose Don
Angelo Roncalli who, it was reported, was the more
"Romanized".

So it happened that at the age of twenty-one, he returned to his native soil as secretary to one of the most
renowned and widely talked about bishops of the day.

If, during the Middle Ages, secular and ecclesiastical
control had very often been vested in members of noble
families, in the nineteenth century and the very first
years of the twentieth, when she had been reorganized to
cope with the secular anti-clerical movement, the Church
placed great reliance upon those great figures who had
exchanged the palace for the Cathedral. Two of them
became Pope; Count Mastai Ferretti, Pius IX, and Count
Pecci, Leo XIII. Others played a large part in the political and social struggles of the time. Von Ketteler, in
Germany, was one, and not dissimilar to him in a
number of ways was Radini-Tedeschi. They had certain

qualities in common; for instance, their permanently youthful and tireless way of tackling problems, their generous and helpful attitude to the aspirations of the workers, and, above all, their lordly refusal to compromise in any way with principles in which they did not believe, even if these principles were a king's own. It wasn't pride, but rather a humble obedience to an inner voice. At times it was excessive modesty, as perhaps in the case of Radini-Tedeschi.

At thirty-three he had been sent for by the Secretary of State, who had noted with satisfaction the book he had just published on international ecclesiastical law.[10] With his intelligence and cultivation – to say nothing of his family and his personal appearance, considerations not unimportant to Leo XIII when making promotions – it had long been certain that he would, one day, be appointed to a high post in the papal diplomatic service.

Finally the Pope offered to send him on a mission to Belgium, but the diplomacy of the time[11] had nothing at all to recommend it to Radini-Tedeschi's tastes and he declined the career offered to him.[12] He was finally appointed to the post of resident canon so that he could remain at the Vatican, to direct the work of those Catholic organizations which so interested him. In four years, first in Rome, and later all over Italy, he worked hard to arouse the

Catholic masses and strike at an antagonistic public opinion. As far as Vatican politics went, he felt more at home with the plans for rebuilding and reconquering Italy for Catholicism than he did with those concerning the defence of the political and territorial claims made by the Holy See.

That the dichotomy was by no means clear to everybody, perhaps not even to those who upheld both sets of aims, may well have been the result of an insufficient knowledge of the very similar state of affairs that had existed in the Middle Ages. If certain pages of medieval history had been properly re-read and considered during those years when the medieval and the gothic were fashionable, perhaps the real nature of contemporary politics might have been more apparent. In the second half of the nineteenth century there was being re-enacted a situation which had arisen in the eleventh and thirteenth centuries, when the Holy See and the State were fiercely opposed. In the Middle Ages the State had been the Holy Roman Empire, now it was the Kingdom of Italy. On both occasions the power of the Pope was being questioned. On the political level they were trying to oust him from temporal power in order, as they declared in both periods, to limit his jurisdiction to exclusively spiritual matters as though he were only a bishop. On an ideological level they were trying to set up against Catholicism another faith and another discipline. In the Middle Ages, they used the very loose term "pataria",[13] in the nineteenth century the term was "progress".

In both periods the Pope's attitude was the same. On the one hand, a judicial vindication of the sovereign rights of the Holy See, and, in consequence, their diplomatic and political vindication against incursions and interferences on the part of the State. On the other hand, the organization of both clergy and laity, in order to oppose, with the controlled strength of a civilized society, any violence on the part of the State.

In the Middle Ages, the twofold achievement of the Popes had been firstly the establishment of a confederation of States of the Church, from the river Po in the North, to Garigliano near Naples, in the South, for the protection of Rome; and secondly, the foundation of a detailed network of Catholic movements and organizations ranging from the different types of lay orders to charitable institutions. Over the last hundred years, the Pope's victories have consisted in the political agreements made with a Catholic Italy, the result of the work done by voluntary movements ranging from religious associations to economic and financial trusts.

A number of medieval Popes, including Gregory VII,

were imprisoned, but this furthered the cause of the State as little as the more recent imprisonment of Pius VI or the confinement of Pius IX in the Vatican.

In considering the Catholic revival in nineteenth century Italy, there is one fact that cannot be overlooked. At the very same time that the secular State was making its final assaults on what territory still remained to the Church, the Pope was beginning to establish throughout the Italian peninsula his great network of Catholic associations, and parish and diocesan committees.[14] Thus all the different social activities were linked together to form a single organism. From that time every year marked a stage forward. Led by a special committee called the Conference Movement, the Catholic congresses were ready for action.

As far as we are aware, people during the Middle Ages were never accused of being either lukewarm or disloyal if they preferred starting a religious society or a charitable institution to making political agreements, forming alliances and going to war to defend the Papal States. In the nineteenth century, however, anyone suggesting that he would rather found a Catholic organization than fight against the new order in any way he could, even if only by boycotting the elections, ran a not inconsiderable risk.[15]

Monsignor Radini-Tedeschi had been in danger a number of times, but he never flinched. He was not a nobleman for nothing. Don Roncalli was, at that time, with him every day, and on every kind of occasion. He learned much, and his character was considerably strengthened as a result of the experience. He wrote of his Bishop: "There was something of the warrior spirit about him. He had to fight for what was good, for the Church, the Pope, the rights of Christian folk. He always chose adequate weapons, preferring to do battle as a true knight, always fairly and openly."[16]

The Bishop's first real clash with the secular power took place soon after he got to Bergamo. This concerned the official visit to the city of Margherita, the Queen Mother. He never failed, however, to behave like a true gentleman.[17]

He again aroused controversy when in 1909 he took sides with the workers on strike. Don Angelo Roncalli took an active part in the business, and later wrote: "The Bishop, who had publicly held aloof from the previous agricultural unrest, was one of the first and most generous of those who contributed money to help the workers when their much publicized strike began in Ranica. This aroused a great deal of indignation, and some ill-disposed reports were even sent to higher quarters. Many right-

26

thinking people thought that a cause should not be supported if any of the means used to achieve its aims were in
danger of being carried to extremes. Monsignor Radini
did not share this point of view. The strike at Ranica was
over a question of principle, and had nothing to do with
wages and working conditions. They had struck over the
fundamental principle of freedom for Christian labor organizations in the face of powerfully organized Capital. The
Bishop had, in this case, taken the worker's side with some
determination, because he felt he was accomplishing a
work of high Christian endeavor, and to use his own
works, "a work of justice, charity and social peace". So he
let the indignation and ill-will towards him continue, and
blithely resumed his course of lively campaign for the
strikers, although he regretted and tried to remedy the
inevitable difficulties and drawbacks that are always to
be expected in such a struggle. The strike lasted a good
seven weeks.[18]

Don Roncalli writes: "And then, when matters were
settled, St. Pius X wrote a personal letter – such was his
habit – to Radini, stating 'I cannot disapprove of what
you, in full knowledge of place, persons and circumstances, deemed it proper to do'".[19]

27

5

FROM LEARNING TO ACTION

DON Roncalli's bishop was as generous with his money as
he was careful with his time. He had the diocese to run,
organizations to manage, inspections to carry out and
many journeys to make, but he never failed to fit in some
hours for study every day – sociology by preference, or
ecclesiastical history. Because he was that sort of man
himself, he lost no time in making it clear that he wanted
his secretary to foster the habit of study also. He entrusted
to Don Roncalli the teaching of ecclesiastical history, in
the diocesan seminary, together with apologetics and the
history of the Church Fathers.

As it happened, he had already felt drawn to these
subjects during the years he had spent in the seminary at
Rome, and had he remained in that city this attraction
might have resulted in his following quite a different
course of life. The study of ecclesiastical history is a means
by which the Catholic is enabled to find his own
rightful place as an individual in that vast organization

which has been living and working for two thousand years. One must agree with the historians when they say that an awareness of one's own individuality and personal responsibility can only be reached through an awareness of one's place in the society in which one lives. If this is true for every educated man who recognizes himself as an integral part of society, how much more valid it is for a Catholic, who knows that he possesses nothing essential or active which does not come to him from the Church.

As a seminarian in Rome, Don Roncalli spent many happy hours poring over the works of Cardinal Cesare Baronius, the man who succeeded St. Philip Neri as the Superior of the Oratorians. In these writings he found much evidence of a life of work and heroism, of changing vicissitudes throughout the centuries; and from his reading he drew the certain consolation of a victory which had always been, and would always be, the reward of clamorous combat and silent suffering.

In his enthusiasm he had already made many notes, but the sheets and notebooks had all been packed hurriedly into his suitcase for the unexpected return to Bergamo. Later, however, while sitting in his room in the seminary, he found time to re-read what he had written. After correcting and amplifying the material he finally decided, with the wholehearted encouragement of his Bishop, to compile from it a book to mark the approaching tercentenary of Baronius. This, his first published work, was entitled *Il Cardinale Cesare Baronio nel terzo centenario della morte*.[20]

The head of the Ambrosian Library in Milan, Dr. Achille Ratti, who had been a friend of the Bishop since the time of his two missions abroad as Papal Legate, now urged Roncalli to undertake a much more copious work. Roncalli himself writes, "I had to accompany Monsignor Radini-Tedeschi to Milan to attend some meetings of the commission which was preparing for the eighth provincial council. These were held in the Archbishop's palace under the direction of the Metropolitan, Cardinal Ferrari, and there were only a few priests taking part. During the hours between meetings, I found nothing more interesting than to visit the extensive archives of the palace, where there were so many unexplored treasures bearing on the history of the Archdiocese of Milan.

"I was immediately struck by a collection of thirty-nine volumes bound in parchment and with 'Spiritual Archives – Bergamo' stamped upon the backs. I explored them, returning again and again. What a wonderful surprise it was to find so many and such interesting documents all gathered together! To read about the Church in Bergamo during the period just after the Council of Trent, when her religious life was being renewed with the burning zeal characteristic of the Catholic counter-Reformation!"[21]

Among the documents there were the reports of the inspection, carried out in 1575, on behalf of the Vatican, both in the city and in the surrounding countryside, by St. Charles Borromeo, who was then a Cardinal. As he read through these forgotten manuscripts, Roncalli felt the ancient Bergamo opening before him; its outlines became more and more clear and, at the same time, so lively and interesting as to seem almost real. There were minutes of trials, testimonies, petitions, decrees, legal controversies, and even the anonymous information of zealous spies. When he had finished, he had a detailed picture of how Bergamo had come through the crisis of the Renaissance.

Did the material merit a more detailed study, or should the idea be allowed to remain a dream? Don Roncalli put the problem before Dr. Ratti and the Bishop.

"Certainly, annotating these manuscripts critically and presenting them within a historical framework would be an excellent thing to undertake", said Dr. Ratti seriously, regarding Don Roncalli with the weak, shortsighted eyes of a man whose life has been spent over faded manuscripts. "An excellent study", he added, "for a *young* man."

There were, in fact, several hundred pounds of documents – enough to keep a man busy for a lifetime![22]

Don Roncalli started by transcribing the texts. It was by no means an easy matter to read them, particularly on account of the curious insertion into the text of passages written in very old dialect and also in old curial Latin. Sometimes his eyes strayed to the indexes in search of information and anecdotes about the places and institutions most dear to his Bergamese heart. This led him to arrive at a conclusion that neither he nor the learned librarian had expected. While he was researching into certain Bergamese ecclesiastical traditions, he found undeniable evidence of the antiquity of the Catholic Action movement for which he was fighting, and which it was thought had been imported into Italy only a few years previously, following suggestions and examples from abroad.[23]

It is certain that he talked to the Bishop about his discovery, if only to obtain his opinion; and once, in 1912, he spoke publicly about it in a lecture on the medieval origins of the welfare activities carried out by the Bergamese Catholics. This lecture was later published, with extensive critical annotations, as a monograph on the *Misericordia Maggiore* and other charitable institutions.[24]

He saw then how Catholic Action had always been

directed at those places "where justice and charity are most manifestly oppressed, so that they might be re-established in the best possible way; but without the illusion that the world can ever become an earthly paradise and without the belief that it will be merely the work of a day".[25] The Bishop was always able to see things as a whole. Roncalli says of him: "His every word was a thought, every thought a welcome directive; all of which together made a masterly program of activity and episcopal government in relation with Catholic Action."[26]

Catholic Action could not be said to have finished when the Conference Movement came to an end, much less to have been forgotten by the men who, like Radini-Tedeschi, devoted their every effort to it. "It was still a very sad subject for him, even after many months, so much had he loved the glorious institution during that intense endeavour he and some of his friends had made to improve its internal structure, and to bend its renewed energies towards the active social welfare necessitated by the changing times."[27]

The crisis of 1907 was therefore met with mature experience and a ready spirit. And yet in the course of that year and the early months of the next, even Bergamo began to feel the influence of a certain "destructive spirit", which was manifest in different places all over the country. It took the form of a "mutual distrust between young and old, an unsureness, a discontent, which inevitably developed, albeit to a much lesser extent than it did everywhere else, into the inexorable and fatal crisis."[28]

But the intervention of the Bishop of Bergamo was prompt and to the point. "The work of reconstruction went ahead efficiently and enthusiastically under his intelligent eye by means of a special temporary commission, until the new statute was ready on December 6.

"On January 15, 1908, a circular was published giving an exact account of the plans which had been worked out during the winter. It presented the new constitution and exhorted Catholics to forget whatever old quarrels they might have and 'with a generous heart and a willing mind' throw themselves, united, into the new work."[29]

And it really was a new work. It was time to pass on from the social and economic fight to the political, which had been rigorously forbidden them for thirty-five years.

It is the history of the *non expedit* – "it is not expedient". It is Bergamese history, as far as the solution of the problem is concerned, because the very first time a Papal veto had been flouted was in Bergamo on the eve of the arrival of the new Bishop, in the Autumn of 1904. It happened when two candidates, well-known Catholics, Piccinelli and Cameroni, stood for Parliament and were elected. In the same election, two other candidates who were known to be Catholics, were elected in Rome and Naples. It seemed like rank disobedience on the part of the electorate, but the reprimand that was feared from the Vatican never came. Instead, an unofficial letter was published in the local Catholic newspaper, justifying the event as the result of an agreement with the Bishops.[30]

In 1904, however, the Catholic Movement had not been able to settle its own programme, either social or political. Participation in the election, like the entry into Parliament, was simply a local expedient to deal with a number of problems which were no more than temporary. Neither might it be said that the Catholics had succeeded in making any political contribution to the State's administrative structure, which had been rebuilt after the renewal of the war of the *Risorgimento*. It was a new structure, the work of new men and new institutions, set up in opposition to the institutions and men who, on the field of battle, in 1848, had sought to realize the vain hopes that had been built up for Italy over the previous two hundred years in the political circles of Italy and Paris.[31]

With the substitution of a secular policy hostile to the Church, for the old traditional one which had been guiding Italy for a thousand years; with the fight openly directed against the Church and Catholic institutions, in

the press and in legislation; with the anti-Catholic terror-
ism, not only against the political leaders of the traditional
regime, but against every individual who did not share
the new ideas; with all this to face in the second half of
the nineteenth century, the Catholics were forced to
withdraw from public life and hold themselves aloof.
"Let none elect and none be elected", was their program in 1862; and now that the archives have begun
to show how dishonestly conducted those elections were,
it may be concluded that, even had they been able to
vote, the Catholics would never have succeeded in making
their desires manifest. So it was that Catholic members
of Parliament like D'Ondes-Reggio and Canossa preferred to abandon their seats after the armed invasion
of Rome by the King's troops. And four years later, in
1874, a strongly-worded decree from the Sacred Apostolic
Penitentiary made abstention from the parliamentary
elections obligatory, declaring that "it was not expedient"
– *non expedit* – to vote in them.

Catholics were encouraged to continue as before, as far
as town and provincial administration was concerned, and
to bring their organizations up to date in order to play their
part in the economic, social and trade union struggles.

Thus, thirty years passed in "abstemious preparation",
as F. Meda calls it, until the Vatican judged that the Catho-

lic Movement was sufficiently powerful in numbers and modern in organization for the battle against anti-Church secularism to begin, both in the field of politics and in legislation.[32] There was a new adversary in sight, socialism, which was beginning to insinuate itself among the masses, who until then had always been faithful and reliable.

The Encyclical, *Fermo Proposito,* of June 11, 1905, set out in detail the possibility of intervention in future parliamentary elections, taking it for granted that the future would see Catholic deputies sitting in Parliament, even if they were not there as direct representatives of the Church. Meanwhile it was left to the bishops to decide whether to ask the Vatican to cancel the *non expedit,* and the Catholic electorate to make all the necessary preparations, so that they might be in a position either to express themselves through their own program, or at least to come to terms with other groups which would guarantee to respect religious and civil traditions.

In Bergamo, the Bishop directed these preparations for four arduous years, in the meantime trying out Catholic strength in the municipal and provincial elections.

"However", writes Don Roncalli, "although the Bishop kept himself extremely well informed about everything, he took very good care not to get himself personally involved in these local elections in any way.

He knew that the capable laymen on the electoral committees were working prudently and sensibly, and he had great faith in them. It did not interest him whether they were rich or poor, he tried always to remain above such considerations. As he said many times in public, it was quite enough for him that Catholics and all men of conscience should see that voting was not only right, but a duty, and that they should remember this most particularly when they were confronted by problems of a religious or moral kind.[33]

The Bergamese certainly knew how to put their discipline and strength to the test.

Apart from this, it was something they had prided themselves upon since 1895, when, thanks to heavy voting, an absolute majority was won in the municipal and provincial elections: with equal obedience these same people abstained from voting in the following parliamentary elections. Thus, with sixty per cent of the voters abstaining, it was impossible even to fill the seats in about twenty of the divisions.[34]

The parliamentary elections of March 1909 were a test case. Twenty-four "Catholic deputies" were returned to Parliament, and even though they were prevented from making any great contribution they still managed to take up a strong ideological position. At the twentieth National

Catholic Congress of 1910, very soon after the elections, their policy was presented and very clearly outlined in a Declaration of Principles against the secularized State, which was already becoming totalitarian, and against "the tendency of the modern State to penetrate into the sanctuary of mind and conscience, setting itself up over the intangible moral and intellectual rights of the spiritual life of the people". It bore the signature of Toniolo.[35]

But even more unmistakable was the victory of the Catholic people themselves in the 1913 elections. Previously, there had been only three million voters, but a new law had been passed which extended the right to vote to all classes. So the electorate was trebled. Naturally, this was a boon to the Socialists, and their numbers in the House swelled very strikingly; but they were not alone in their success, for the number of Catholic seats was doubled and approximately forty Catholic deputies took their seats.[36]

Nevertheless, it was still not possible for a qualified parliamentary group to be established by the Catholics because, as such, they would have had to face the problem of the legitimacy of the national institutions, but this did not mean that they were prevented from stating their program. Quite the opposite, in fact, for this point had been clearly dealt with in the anticipatory warning already issued in February and again in May by Count

Della Torre, the new president of the then largest Catholic association, the People's Union. The Catholic electorate, he declared, had its own program to carry out: a popular program aimed at the social good.[37]

The news put new heart into the young. As things then stood, there was a growing fear that more and more people would lose interest, because it was not obvious to them that the Catholic Movement had the strength to put its ideals into practice. This movement was, however, already mature and ready to fight – as at Bergamo, for example – so that it was now possible to put up candidates who had a clear conception of the program, and who would know how to fight Socialism with the most modern and efficient weapons.

In Bergamo, the Bishop drew strength from his experiences as a sociologist and organizer. He approved and supported the program drawn up by the electoral committee, on which Don Roncalli and Rezzara were now working together. Giuseppe Belotti[38] states that this program required that "for certain constituencies, candidates should be chosen who are more alive to social questions and who will stand firm on matters of principle". This request resulted in Rezzara being attacked by his opponents and by those who had never been able to forgive him for his victory in the Ranica strike of 1909.

They said he was running before he could walk, even disobeying Vatican instructions; and in Rome so much attention was given to these accusations that the Union of Electors, contrary to the instructions of the People's Union, prepared a disavowal of the program to be published as an article in *L'Osservatore Romano*. Finally, the Bishop of Bergamo intervened himself.

The Bishop, now very ill in Rome, and about to return to Bergamo, begged an audience at the Vatican the moment he heard of the impending publication of the article. He talked, making them listen to him, until finally he convinced them. But the strain was to hasten his death, for he was worn out by bitterness and fatigue.

"Undoubtedly, my dear Rezzara", he wrote from Rome, "someone has been trying to interfere in the running of the diocese, as though we were doing things contrary to pontifical orders. It is overwhelmingly sad. But I have not failed to let them know the truth, and clear matters up."[39]

After his return to Bergamo, the illness that was wearing him out became worse. For some time a private grief had been sapping his strength and it was not long before he died in the arms of Don Angelo on August 22, 1914, invoking peace upon men at a time when war had already been let loose in the world.[40]

6

THE APOSTLE OF YOUTH

Don Roncalli was now alone. His Bishop had died in
his arms, overwhelmed with the grief and the pain of
seeing the war looming up so inexorably over the world.
And now that same war was taking away his friends and
colleagues who had fought the social and political battles
with him. Everyone was going away.

They all came to bid him farewell, wearing awkward-
looking gray-green capes and hobnailed boots that echoed
down the quiet corridors of the seminary; then off they
went, far away, over the mountains.

Don Roncalli, too, was expecting to be drafted, and
his turn came on at Pentecost. He had already done one
year's military service, in 1902, as an ordinary soldier in
Bergamo, interrupting his studies in Rome to do so.
He served in the 73rd Infantry Regiment which was
part of the Lombardy Brigade, and when discharged had
attained the rank of sergeant.

Now he travelled home to Sotto il Monte still wearing

his cassock, said farewell to his family, and went to Milan.

In 1915, military regulations stipulated that all priests drafted were to be enrolled in the medical corps. Don Roncalli was no exception, and he reported to the military hospital of San Ambrogio in Milan – a building which stood on the same site as that now occupied by the impressive Catholic university buildings. He was immediately given the rank of sergeant and then dispatched to the military hospital at Bergamo. Thus he was able to be near the wounded and dying, to sit at the bedside of those who came back broken, maimed and sick with pain and despair.

Although at first he had been a sergeant he was later appointed chaplain[41] and for four years went round day after day, from one hospital to another, looking not only at the unshaved and bandaged faces of the men, but also deeper down into their hearts and souls. Many of them were tortured by terrible memories of bayonet warfare, by the vision of the men they had killed for no other reason than that they wore a uniform of a different colour and spoke another language.

He must have learned far more about truth and reality from the words of the men dying in the hospitals than from the pages of his theology books, yet these were a solace and perhaps a type of refuge for him. In the evenings, frequently far into the night, with the icy detachment of the scholar, he continued his task of cataloguing the sixteenth-century Bergamese documents he had discovered in the Ambrosian Library – but how far off now seemed the happy mornings spent working there. This task completed, he devoted his energies to writing the biography of the late Bishop Radini-Tedeschi.

Once, almost out of a sense of duty, he accepted the seminary's invitation to give a series of lectures to the advanced students on apologetics. But one by one they too went away to the war, until in the Spring there remained only three or four. To these he smilingly presented the folders containing all his old notes on the subject.

Peace came at last and brought with it a sense of wistful regret that Radini-Tedeschi had not lived to see the landslide in favour of Catholic social and political ideas, a landslide which had been set in motion by Pope Benedict XV, the late Bishop's friend. Who of the pioneers was now left? Rezzara also was dead, and there were many others who had gone to the war never to return.

Don Roncalli moved to the ancient Marenzi Palace, where the new Bishop of Bergamo, Monsignor Marelli, had given him permission to start a students' hostel. His position as a seminary professor was now exchanged for the higher and more responsible one of spiritual director of the theology students who had just returned from the war and wished to recommence their studies for the priesthood.

In December 1920 he was called to Rome by Benedict XV to help in the reorganization of the Catholic missions. His work took him on visits of inspection to Belgium, Holland, Germany and France. In the following March, he was appointed to be President of the Italian branch of the Society for the Propagation of the Faith, and in May was made a Domestic Prelate.

It was not long before he came to the notice of Pope Pius XI, who recognized him as the meticulous researcher and careful scholar he had known in the Ambrosian Library. He was appointed Italian member of the General High Council of the Pontifical Society for the Propagation of the Faith. Later, Pope Pius XI made him a member of the committee that was busy preparing the Missionary Exhibition to be held during the coming Holy Year. At the same time he held the post of Professor of Patrology at the Roman Seminary.

In March 1924 Pius XI sent him for a short time to France.

France still possessed something of the crusading spirit

– she was the home of men who became missionaries in the desert, freed slaves, and who worked with lepers. To the Italian she was quiet, hard-working and intense; so that she seemed to be a white-hot spiritual forge, and it was during this time that Monsignor Roncalli first became aware of his growing love for the country in which he was later to reside as Nuncio.

7

THE FIRST MISSIONS

In order to expedite preparations for the Holy Year, Pius XI decided to take a personal interest in the complicated procedure. Two years before, he had issued general specifications to be followed in the planning of a Missionary Exhibition. These he re-emphasized in his speech to the Cardinals on May 23, 1923. The following year on January 24, the Catholic Action set up a special committee and, in Fall 1924 the organizers set to work and did an excellent job. Pius XI was highly pleased and praised their industry.

The Pope wanted to be kept continually informed concerning the progress of the work – this, too, was a usual habit of his – and while following the preparations for the Holy Year, he also observed the way in which Monsignor Roncalli was handling the arrangements for the Missionary Exhibition. He observed again that same diligence and perseverance which he had first noted in the Ambrosian Library, and that Monsignor Roncalli still worked with the same unflagging spirit in everything he did. Philology, history, the discharge of his duties at the offices of the Congregation for the Propagation of the Faith, which was in charge of all missionary work, teaching, and now in the daily contacts he had with the world's press about the Exhibition which was arousing the interest of reporters and scholars alike. Pius XI therefore decided to trust this earnest and painstaking Bergamese with a task that was both difficult and delicate.

After the signing of the Treaty of Neuilly someone had to visit Bulgaria to find out the true nature of the situation there among Catholics of both the Latin and Byzantine rites with a view to solving any problems. Bulgarian Catholics, who were a minority in a largely Orthodox population, were passing through a difficult crisis, and the whole nation was in a state of general disorder characterized by local uprisings, military plots, the revival of old movements such as the O.R.I.M. (revolutionary committees aiming at the separation of the Macedonian territories from Bulgaria), and the infiltration of Bolshevik secret agents. The Bulgarian religious situation was equally difficult. The schism between the Bulgarian and the Greek Orthodox Churches still existed in 1925, the final result of the independent Exarchate of 1860, which was recognized by the Porte ten years later since the

Bulgarians still formed part of the Turkish Empire. In their 1872 Synod, the Greek Orthodox Church condemned such nationalism on the part of the Slavs and excommunicated the Bulgarians. This excommunication, however, was not recognized by the other Orthodox Churches, who remained in communion with both Bulgarians and Greeks. The schism was real, however, and during the Balkan Wars (1912–13) the Exarch moved from Constantinople to Sofia, where he died in 1916. He was succeeded collectively by the Synod under the Metropolitan of Sofia. Thus the Bulgarian Orthodox Church became more independent. Even so, the times were very different from those of Innocent III, when Basil had been able to request the title of Primate, so that Bulgaria, then independent, should be clearly seen and acknowledged as something separate from the Eastern Roman Empire. The ruined and embittered Bulgarian nation that issued from the Treaty of Neuilly could no longer trust anyone, perhaps not even itself.

For the Roman Catholics of Bulgaria Rome had, in 1883, set up a Vicariate Apostolic in Macedonia, and another in Thrace. The provisions of the Treaty of Neuilly in 1919, by which Greece and Rumania acquired territory formerly part of Bulgaria, created new problems.

Considering the especially explosive national feelings of the Balkan peoples, it is very dangerous when ecclesiastical districts of jurisdiction do not coincide with national boundaries. Furthermore, a great many Catholics of the Byzantine rite had emigrated from the surrendered districts of Thrace and Macedonia to what was left of Bulgaria, where their religious needs had to be cared for. Thus there was an urgent need for ecclesiastical reorganization in this part of the world.

Thirty years previously the Bulgarian Catholics had had a leader at the Ottoman Court. He died in 1923, old and weighed down by the terrible confusion of the wars, the diplomatic "peaces", and the recent rioting. The Vatican had established a religious center in Sofia under a single Apostolic Administrator. But no sooner had one been appointed in the Spring of 1925 than he died, unconsecrated. Monsignor Roncalli's visit took place soon afterwards.

In March 3, 1925 Monsignor Roncalli was appointed titular Bishop of Areopolis, with the title of Archbishop, and Apostolic Visitor to Bulgaria. He was consecrated in the church of San Carlo on the Corso, on March 19, by Cardinal Tacci, Secretary to the Congregation for the Eastern Church. The Archbishops Palica and Marchetti-Salvaggiani assisted. His first Mass as a bishop was offered

50

at the altar of the Confession in St. Peter's where he had offered his first Mass as a priest.

Archbishop Roncalli's first task was to find a successor for the lately dead Apostolic Administrator. After considering the matter carefully for some months, he put forward the name of a thirty-four-year-old priest, Kyrill Kurteff, who was appointed during 1926 and took up his duties at the end of that year. No better choice could have been made. Kurteff, now Exarch, bravely remained at his post when Communist persecutions swept the country. Only a few months ago, he was arrested and imprisoned. The same fate lay in store for some of his fellow prelates – Monsignor Eugene Romanoff, whom Archbishop Roncalli appointed Vicar Apostolic of Sofia and Philippopolis, and Monsignor Eugene Bussilkoff, a Passionist, who was made Bishop of Nicopolis in 1947, only to be immediately imprisoned without trial, and, in 1951, condemned to death, since when nothing has been heard of him. In 1925, however, these events could not be foreseen although an unfavorable omen for the future was the Communist bomb-throwing in Sofia Orthodox Cathedral.

According to the official report that Archbishop Roncalli made to Pius XI during a brief visit to Rome[42], there were 45,000 Bulgarian Catholics of both rites.

Three or four years later this number had increased to 47,000.[43] 40,000 of them, Catholics from old Thracian and Macedonian families, were divided between the diocese of Nicopolis, immediately answerable to the Pope, and the Vicariate Apostolic of Sofia-Philippopolis, both of which followed the Paulician (or Westernized) rite. The remaining 7,000 Bulgarian Catholics, of the Slav-Byzantine rite, had only an Apostolic Administrator. Archbishop Roncalli took action, therefore, in order that these Catholics of the Eastern Rite might have their own hierarchical organization, and in 1926 he got the Vatican to establish the Exarchate of Sofia. (Kurteff, whom he had so greatly esteemed ever since his first days in Sofia, was nominated to it in 1941.) But this was not all; after he had appointed the Byzantine Bishop Ordinant, Archbishop Roncalli had to think about providing the future priests. He founded a Jesuit seminary, the first to be founded there for hundreds of years.

The Vatican, pleased with his work, converted his mission from a temporary to a permanent one. In 1931 he was appointed the first Apostolic Delegate Bulgaria had ever had.

Apostolic Delegates, according to Canon Law, "are Papal Representatives without diplomatic status"; that is to say, they are accredited only to the episcopate of the country they are sent to, and this is usually a non-Catholic, sometimes a non-Christian country, preferring not to have relations with the Vatican.[44] There was, therefore, never any reason why Archbishop Roncalli should go to the royal palace. He never, for example, had any credentials to present to the King. But once, before his appointment as Apostolic Delegate, he was sent for in order to deal with the formalities connected with the wedding between the Orthodox Boris III and Princess Giovanna of Savoy, a Catholic. The Church's law concerning mixed marriages applies as equally in Sofia as it does in Rome, and as this was to be a mixed marriage, permission was only granted on condition that the wedding ceremony took place in a Catholic church, and that any children, boys or girls, should be brought up as Catholics. The King gave his solemn promise, and the wedding took place in Assisi, Italy, during a terrible storm. Then, contrary to the oaths that Boris had sworn, services – and later baptisms – took place in Sofia Orthodox Cathedral.

The first protest, concerning the Orthodox baptism of the first child, Princess Marie Louise, was made "through official channels".[45] The Pope's personal protest, however, made before the Cardinals in Consistory on March 13, 1933, was more violent. He denied all rumors of political interference, and declared that he had negotiated with "the sovereigns themselves, and with them only".[46] The wretched queen was spared all blame and any ecclesiastical condemnation, because Archbishop Roncalli, in Sofia, had laid bare evidence of intrigue, and had even managed to speak to her. "We have irrefutable evidence to show where the responsibility lies", asserted Pius XI, and he did not forbear to utter words of comfort for "an indeed afflicted mother, protesting her innocence in everything that had occurred: she had nothing to do with it, and has in no way given her consent to it".

Apart from this affair with its disagreeable political overtones, Archbishop Roncalli succeeded in maintaining friendly social and diplomatic relations in Bulgaria. In November 1926, for example, there took place on religiously neutral ground, the Officers' Club in the capital, a gathering in celebration of the centenary of the Council of Nicaea. The French and Polish ministers and the Secretary to the Czech Legation, as well as members of the municipal administration of Sofia, were present at this occasion.[47]

As Apostolic Delegate he stayed another three years in Bulgaria, strengthening the links with the Holy See, and rebuilding the organization of both the Catholic rites. Like all foreigners in Bulgaria, perhaps the most generous and hospitable country in Europe[48], he always felt himself among friends, but just as he was beginning to settle down there he was commissioned with an even more delicate task. It was announced that he had been appointed Apostolic Delegate to Turkey and Greece.[49] He arrived in Istanbul early in January, 1935.

In the new republic of Turkey they were putting into effect the Treaties of Locarno and Ankara, with the result that a million Greeks were in process of being moved out of Turkey, and half that number of Turks out of Greece. In addition, this exchange of population had repercussions on the Greek religious situation, for there were a large group of Greek Catholics among the people being repatriated from Istanbul and Anatolia who, for many generations, had been living their own traditional lives under the rule of their bishop, enjoying the local autonomy and light taxation typical of territories on the outer fringes of the Ottoman Empire.

When, however, this independent Catholicism was bodily transferred from the cosmopolitan environment of Turkey, and set down within the compact Orthodoxy of Greece, there was bound to be trouble. There had been a Latin Catholic Cathedral in Athens since the end of the nineteenth century to look after the spiritual welfare of the descendants of those medieval merchants who had come from Genoa, Venice, Pisa and Amalfi to settle in the archipelago. The only clue to their origin was to be found in their names and their religion. Numbering only a few thousand, they were looked upon almost as a sort of ethnic curiosity, and in no wise clashed with the real Hellenism of the prevailing Orthodoxy. When, however, yet another Cathedral came to be built for the Byzantine Catholics that arrived in 1923 it was considered the thin end of the wedge that would split the national unity that the ancient Orthodox faith afforded. It was regarded with even greater suspicion than was the opening of Latin Rite Schools in the middle of the nineteenth century, a suspicion that was reflected in the 1938 Law, which, on Archbishop Roncalli's arrival, was still being worked out in the Greek Parliament, and which demonstrated the steadfast opposition to any parliamentary attempt to open diplomatic relations with the Vatican. Politically, Greek sympathies have always lain with England, and this sympathy has also had its effect on the policy of the Orthodox Church which, in 1920, 1930, 1948, and 1958, sent delegates to the Lambeth Conference in England, and in 1938 to the Ecumenical Congress at Edinburgh. They have also recognized the validity of Anglican ordinations.[50]

This brief description of the situation shows how difficult was the task with which Archbishop Roncalli had been entrusted, even though, as has been mentioned, an

Apostolic Delegate is accredited only to the episcopate of that country to which he is sent.

From Istanbul he visited Athens, and on his arrival there tried to disperse any illwill that the Orthodox might be feeling. At that time there was a strong anti-Bulgarian feeling in Greece. Nobody there had been able to forget the League of Nations' intervention forcing the Greeks to evacuate the town of Petrik on the Bulgarian frontier, which they had occupied in 1925. They feared Bulgaria's growing strength, a result of the active part King Boris was playing in politics. He had suppressed the Macedonian revolutionary movement, asked Kiosseivanoff to form a government, and concluded the so-called Military Alliance with Italy. February 1934 had seen the drawing-up of the Balkan *Entente,* apparently against Bulgaria, which Paris had planned as a continuation of the Little *Entente*. Under these circumstances the announcement that Archbishop Roncalli, until recently the Vatican's representative in Sofia, had been appointed Apostolic Delegate to Greece as well as Turkey caused considerable alarm throughout Greece.

He therefore remained in his house in Odos Omirou, leaving it only to visit the various Catholic communities. In addition, he always combined these visits with the celebration of some kind of religious service. He was frank and friendly towards the Orthodox, and showed the greatest admiration for the recent revival of their ancient apostolic zeal not only in their public charities, but in their cultural activities also.[51]

During the tragic days of 1941–44, of war and military occupation, the Greeks found in Archbishop Roncalli the only man who could, or would, do anything vigorous to speed up the sending of food supplies, medicine and clothing. The Apostolic Delegate was asked by Greek politicians and dignitaries of the Orthodox Church to approach the Vatican. He thereupon went straight to Rome in order to ask the Pope to approach the Allied governments about opening a way through the blockade against Greece. Pius XII was, in fact, able to arrange for food to be sent to Greece to relieve the hungry. This the Greeks have never forgotten.[52]

He strove successfully on behalf of the Jews, too, doing everything that lay in his power to prevent their being deported.[53]

Even though it was an uphill struggle for him, he stood firm in upholding the rights of the two thousand or so Byzantine Catholics to continue to live according to their rites and under their Exarch. He hoped that time and events would prove that the Byzantine Cathedral in Athens had not been set up with any intention of proselytizing, much less to create a schism, and it seems now that time and events are indeed on his side. He had the same hopes concerning the pro-cathedral of Beyoglu, Istanbul.

The last vicissitudes of the Byzantine Catholics of Greece may be said to have begun at the time of the Balkan Wars. In 1911, the Vatican had been obliged to dissolve two new orders, one for men, the other for women, which had started without sufficient funds, but it founded an episcopal administration for the Greeks in the territory administered by the Istanbul Apostolic Delegation. At that time it was in charge of the same Monsignor Tacci who later became Cardinal and Secretary to the Congregation for the Eastern Church, and who was to consecrate the then Monsignor Roncalli as Bishop in 1925 before he left for Bulgaria.

What appreciably altered the situation was the First World War, with its subsequent treaties. The inhabitants of Malgara and Dandelion, two villages in Thrace, which had seen a reawakening of Catholicism since 1882, were now being evicted and moved to Salonika; on the other hand, many Byzantine Catholics in Istanbul were being shifted to Athens. Consequent upon this movement, the Byzantine bishop extended his jurisdiction over the whole of Greece in 1925, reorganizing the seminary, the schools, an orphanage, a religious order for women – the Panmaca-ristos nuns – and some Catholic Action societies. This extension of jurisdiction led to the already mentioned reactions of the Greek Orthodox block, which until then had been erratic, and which Archbishop Roncalli succeeded in moderating by his prudent reserve and through the prestige he gained in the war.

Following the same policy of respecting the cultural rights of every minority, however small, he gave generous help to the three thousand or so Armenians who, over the years, had emigrated from their stricken land and come to start a new life in Greece.[54] In giving them an eccle-siastical organization he acted with great consideration for the sensitivity of the Eastern Church; a consideration, perhaps, not fully appreciated by some in Orthodox circles. A separate Greek diocese was constituted only for those Armenians living in Greece, leaving those in Istanbul under their bishop in Asia, whereas all Greek Catholics, whether living in Greece or in European Turkey, were placed under one bishop who had his Cathedral in Athens. "For the capital of Greece is the true capital of Hellenism", as it was officially put in a Vatican document of the time.[55]

Rome's expressed fondness for Athens surely made no easier Archbishop Roncalli's relations with Turkey, where

Kemal Ataturk's republic, proclaimed in 1923, had inherited from the sultans a motley collection of peoples. In Istanbul the Catholic population alone was made up of the following diversified groups: Latin Catholics, principally Italian and French; Syrian Catholics, the descendants of the ancient Jacobites who were patronized by the Empress Theodora, and the descendants of those who had come during the periods of the crusades; Chaldean Catholics, that is, Christians originally of Mediterranean stock who had returned to Europe from places as far distant as China and Malabar; and lastly Armenian Catholics. The Apostolic Delegate, who is the Vatican representative in this multi-racial Catholic community, is, at the same time, Administrator of the Latin Rite Vicariate of Constantinople and, therefore, the immediate religious leader of the Latin Catholic community there.[56]

Archbishop Roncalli had no opportunity to be idle during this period. In addition to all his other duties it was the accepted thing that the Apostolic Delegate might also have access to the Turkish Government in the event of there being any state business to transact. Although he could act only in a private and unofficial capacity, the burden of work involved was not, because of this, lightened.

Kemal Ataturk's policy was directed towards the

rapid development of Turkish youth: it was nationalism with a vengeance, a reaction against the thousand-year-old traditions of the Levant coupled with an even, at times, violent drive towards westernization. The Swiss code of Laws was hurriedly adopted; the wearing of the fez, the Caliphate, the Arabic alphabet, Friday holidays, the Hejiric reckoning, and polygamy were all abolished. Reason and enlightenment came like a mighty wave to break against the rocky coast of Anatolia and the pearly enchantment of the Bosporus.

In ten years, illiteracy decreased from 93 to 63 per cent, but the republic that had started free compulsory schooling everywhere closed all the schools run by Western monks and nuns, together with the Koranic schools run by the mosques. In addition, when the constitution was reformed in April 1928, the National Assembly passed a law in virtue of which Islam ceased to be the state religion of the republic. During the Second World War, Turkey remained uncompromisingly neutral and maintained a policy of frosty politeness towards other nations. She was opposed to making any concessions, and the only power that could hope to negotiate with her was the Vatican. This was perhaps because anti-Catholicism lessened somewhat after the death of Ataturk. In any case the Apostolic Delegate did have a certain amount of diplomatic success. His neutrality was beyond all suspicion, likewise his clear understanding of the points of view of belligerent groups.[57]

The Vatican first became anxious about the Turkish schools question in 1924. Cardinal Gasparri at once despatched Monsignor Dolci to Ankara. Known as "the friend of the Turks", he was the last Apostolic Delegate to present his credentials to the Sultan,[58] and now held the post of Nuncio in Bucharest. He was received by his old friend, Vassiv Bey, now Minister of Education, whom he asked: "What would the Government have to say to somebody proposing to open his own schools in Istanbul for the twelve hundred children left without one? And supposing that somebody were I, Angelo Dolci?" Vassiv Bey replied: "We must not speak of religious schools, either Catholic or otherwise, and we certainly must not speak of Italian or French schools. But we could talk of Angelo Dolci schools." They understood one another at once. Five schools were needed in Constantinople, and five were permitted. A simple, yet legal, way had been found.

A lightening perception of situations and witty simple solutions are especially likely to bring success in the Orient. Another anecdote tells how Dolci won over, at a stroke, the unbending Kemal Ataturk with a timely jest.

When Dolci had to make his Nuncial visits to the President, he always dressed like an ordinary priest, as the law insisting on the wearing of civilian dress had not at that time been passed. One morning, however, hardly had he begun to speak than Kemal broke in with more than his usual bluntness. "What are you wearing on your head?" he asked. Dolci had been in such a hurry that he had forgotten to take off his purple skull cap. He removed it, showed it to the dictator, and smilingly answered, "It is a kind of fez that we priests wear when we are visiting and wish to make a special gesture of honor towards our host."

Archbishop Roncalli quickly managed to obtain the goodwill of the Government, the press and the people by means of a translation consisting of only a few sentences. It happened in this way. After his arrival in Istanbul he went one evening to visit one of the Latin churches there, in Galatia, not far from the Delegation. We have already mentioned how he always liked to combine his visits of inspection with a service. On this occasion, as he walked in procession back to the sacristy, he heard people in their pews reciting a prayer in French. Asking the reason for this, he was told that they had always done so, perhaps because French was the one modern language that everybody in the Levant could understand. "But is the flock French?" he persisted. "No, they are all Turks."

"Well then, surely it would be better to have it trans-
lated into Turkish?" He asked for an educated man and
explained to him the meaning of the more difficult
sentences. The next Sunday, the whole congregation was
able to read the prayer in its own language, for it had
been printed during the week. As this was the language
that Kemal Ataturk was substituting for Arabic, even in
the Muezzin's proclamations, it was natural that Roncalli's
"sympathy" should be widely extolled, with the result
that it was no longer easy for the Government to refuse
him requests.

But another evening was to arrive when translation of
another kind would keep him busy. Nine years went by,
and he was re-reading a poem written in 1138, by another
Bergamese, who, like himself, had landed in Turkey. It was
the *Laudes Bergami* by Mosè del Brolo:

> *Hinc praetercurrunt duo flumina gurgite miro*
> *Montibus ex altis orientia murmure diro*
> *Serius a solis nascentis labitur ora*
> *Brembus ab occidua quatinus resonantia lora . . .*

Arising from the mountains high with gloomy roar,
Two rushing torrents from this spot do pour,
Down on the eastern side the Serio goes
With sharp whip cracks the Brembo westward flows.

It might have been applied to Turkey – the Bosporus to the east and the Golden Horn to the west – but the river Serio and the river Brembo are something quite different. He looked out of the windows at the eastern sky over Uskudar, the Bosporus and Galatia – and it was as if, beyond the wide Pangalti Avenue, he could see the skies of his own Lombardy. Christmas was fast approaching with its arduous ceremonies and increased diplomatic activity. Suddenly he was brought a telegram from the Vatican. It was set in code and read: 284145 stop 416564 stop 855003 stop 641100 stop. With the aid of his code-book he tried to decipher it. Could this really be true? He checked it two or three times. There could be no mistake, it read: "Return immediately. Transferred Nuncio Paris, Tardini."

8

IN FRANCE

THE new Nuncio arrived in Paris on the evening of December 30, and among the bustling crowd that got off the train in the grimy darkness of the Gare de Lyon he looked just like any other priest. He had been officially appointed Nuncio on the 22nd., and so had had only seven short days to learn something about the situation with which he was expected to cope. He had sat working at his desk in the Vatican far into the night, and managed to assimilate all the more indispensable material. He spent two more nights over the papers he found waiting for him in Paris. The very first dawn of 1945, which came creeping across the garden of 10 Avenue Wilson, found him just about to go to bed for an hour or two. He had to present his credentials at 9.45 am.

The President of the temporary Government, General Charles de Gaulle, was accompanied by the Foreign Minister, M. Bidault, and M. Loze. If the Nuncio had not hurried to get there, his place at the head of the diplomatic corps would have been taken, after half an hour, by the Russian Ambassador who would have delivered the formal New Year address in his place. Therefore the promptness of Archbishop Roncalli's appearance might even be explained by the fact that ambassadors and ministers plenipotentiary had begun to arrive early and were arranging themselves in order of precedence in the Armour Room. At their head stood the Russian Ambassador, rolling and unrolling the speech which had been sent from Moscow for the occasion by special air courier. Then suddenly the new Nuncio entered.

Archbishop Roncalli simply put himself at their head and began the official address to de Gaulle, who had entered by a door opposite. He read:

"Mr. President, inexpressible trials and sufferings have marked these last years for France but, thanks to your energy and clearsighted policy, she has again found liberty, and confidence in her own destiny." De Gaulle could, of course, only agree with this, and it made a good basis for their future relations. With these words the Nuncio had expressed a note of confidence which was a source of great, though as yet unformulated hope for France, at a time when war was still raging throughout her territories, and when the problems of national reconstruction and those of domestic politics, were still unsolved.[59]

The outstanding problem in France at that time, one which occupied all Frenchmen, was to determine the guilt of those who had adhered to the Vichy government. According to the extremists it meant no less than collaboration with the enemy. Now Hervé, wanting to cure the French people of their addiction to the drug of religion, wrote wittily in *Humanité* suggesting that at least half of the eighty-seven members of the hierarchy should be dismissed, because, he maintained, they had co-operated with the invader.

At the Quai d'Orsay, they were altogether less vehement in their demands and were prepared to be satisfied if only thirty-three bishops were removed. Since the Foreign Minister, Bidault, was a Catholic, General de Gaulle took charge of the matter personally.[60] When the Nuncio came to talk to him about it for the first time and heard the request for the removal of thirty-three Bishops, he slowly opened the dossier he had been given, went through it, shut it up again, looked hard into the other's eyes, and said, "I see only newspaper cuttings here. Would you please show me the evidence against the accused?"

This had to be collected, assessed, examined and re-examined with the Nuncio. All this took about ten months and, in the end, it was agreed that only three bishops should be withdrawn.[61] Naturally the communists were far from satisfied and kept up the accusations.

In the next crisis, over money for Catholic schools, people of all classes joined in opposing the Church. In these arguments the traditional logic of the French seemed to be entirely lacking.

In democratic countries, so the Catholics argued, the sum of the taxes collected for educational purposes should be distributed among all schools, whether private or public. They affirmed, and still do, that the way in which the money was shared out should depend on the way each school functioned, the number of its pupils and teachers, and above all the standard of its success in public examinations. In effect, however, the government gave to the private schools only a small share of all the money received. In France, 1,700,000 children go to private schools, and of this number the great majority are Catholics, comprising 22 per cent of those attending school.[62]

In Paris there are many people who prefer the scents of the Rue de la Paix to the smell of incense, and, when the constitution was being re-drafted, these joined with the communists and socialists in an effort to get all government help to private schools stopped, since the majority of these are run by religious. The argument still continues in the French Parliament today; it flared up in 1951 and

1956, but it was at its very worst during the first years of Archbishop Roncalli's Nunciature. The Bishops always affirmed, right from their first collective pastoral in March 1945, that "the mission of the State is not to teach a single doctrine in a single school". A year afterwards, the M. R. P. group proposed to the Constituent Assembly liberty of education, but the constitution of the newborn state did not sanction this principle. It was then that the Bishops issued another collective pastoral in which they once more made an appeal for this liberty, one among the many which people had been proclaiming for years in order to try to justify all the slaughter of the war. The obvious reaction of the communists was, "the Bishops do not want to obey the law now and make the excuse that human law cannot prevail against divine, but during the occupation they always advised us to obey the authorities".[63]

So the struggle began all over again, only this time it was worse. One minister let himself go against the clergy and was reported in the popular press. The result was that everywhere there was talk of "Popish plotting in the monasteries, the last refuge of murderers and traitors". From the pulpit of Notre Dame, Father Riquet denounced the "base calumnies spoken by some popular parties and by the hardened elements of pre-war anti-clericalism".

This was in March 1947, and about the same time there appeared in the columns of *La Croix* an open letter to the head of the Government, written by Riquet and signed 'Knight of the Legion of Honor, Resistance Medal, Freedom Medal for Exceptional Services, Vice President of the National Federation of Internees and Deportees'. It contained the following sentence: "That, before he has even proved the treason, a minister should feed public opinion with isolated facts, which, by the time they have been fully exploited by the gutter press are sufficient to sully the name of every priest in France, is nothing short of libel."

Finding itself faced with this offensive, the episcopate, having co-ordinated its policy with Roncalli's, stood firm by the principles declared in the spring of 1945: "The Church demands nothing from the State but respect for her independence and the possibility of carrying out her spiritual and social mission efficiently; she still acts on these principles and she always will, whatever may be the all-too-human changes among governments and institutions." It was also declared that: "In a sphere quite distinct from the field in which Catholic Action operates, Catholics should immediately take personal responsibility for their actions as citizens."

This, then, was the policy of the whole French hierarchy and it was certainly supported by the Nuncio. In France, however, the episcopate possessed such authority and civic pride that it was perfectly capable of fighting the battle for its constitutional rights with dignity and absolute decision.

The Nuncio tried to avoid showing himself at the Foreign Office, visiting it only when not to do so was impossible. In fact he delivered only one memorandum in eight years and then it was a case of necessity. "I don't like red tape", he would explain with a smile, and when Dumaine, the Chief of Protocol, expressed surprise at receiving him so rarely, Archbishop Roncalli briefly outlined his reasons: "I come to see the members of your Government as seldom as possible – usually only when they particularly want to see me. M. Bidault himself has reproached me for coming so seldom. Admittedly when Cardinal Ferrata was Nuncio in France at the beginning of the century, he went down to the Quai d'Orsay every week; but the ministers at that time were really adversaries of the Church, and the Nuncio had to make his presence felt. But that isn't the case with me. I find myself among friends, and I've no wish at all to compromise any of them."

He was a master of the art of detachment, being well able to keep himself apart and yet remain alert and watchful. In the Nuncio's residence one evening, Schuman remarked to another guest, "No one of us possesses what he's got — that detachment. Just look at him. He's the only man in the whole of Paris who carries peace around with him. You've only got to be near him and you can breathe it — touch it too, I'd almost say."

And yet according to Pinay, the Nuncio never refused any invitation, nor did he miss an opportunity of giving one. He was for ever out and about in Paris or making trips up and down France. He nearly always went on foot, for it was his intention to get to know, by means of personal contact with the people, the true conditions in France. He went for long walks along the embankments or through the little streets around the boulevards; he might have been found on the steps of Montmartre or gazing into some left-bank gallery window; sometimes he stopped to browse in the bookshops on the Place de l'Opéra and sometimes to call at one of the butchers' in the Rue de la Seine or Rue d'Assas, where he often had occasion to go since the headquarters of French Catholicism was in that area.

He was not unaware, therefore, of the sorry condition of the working class, nor of the perhaps still more squalid lot of the peasants whom he carefully questioned whenever he made a trip into the country. The poverty of the work-

ing man and, above all, his inner misery, a mixture of
desolation, fear and rancour, were as obvious to Archbishop
Roncalli as to any of the French Bishops. Regarding strikes,
he probably had more experience than most, and he knew
what happened to a home when the wages stopped
coming in. In Bergamo he had taken money and parcels
of food to the wives of the strikers, and he had felt for
himself the chill of those bleak houses. As a result he could
do no other than approve wholeheartedly all the bishops
did for the strikers' families in December 1948.[64]

From the same point of view and with the same feelings,
he had supported the Bishops on another question of
humanity and justice, that of restoring to their families
the innocent people who were still in prison charged with
collaboration. The war had been over for two years and
still there were thousands of women, children and old people waiting for the return of these, yet untried, prisoners.

President Auriol received a petition from the bishops in
which it was hoped that some way might be found "to
put an end to the uncertainty and anguish of so many
French families, caused by the penal proceedings arising out
of the war." At the same time they begged for more
human conditions for German prisoners of war in
French camps.

Already, in June 1946, Pius XII had proclaimed before

the Consistory that there existed "sacred rights which cry out to Heaven, higher and stronger than any man-made law". But a year had passed since these words were spoken and the German prisoners in France still numbered over 260,000. No doubt they were well treated, but should they, any longer, be forced to work far from their homes and families; from homes that had been bombed, from families that had been broken or violated? The Cardinals and Bishops of France, finding that those in power would not listen to them, made, on March 23, 1948, a second and supreme appeal, this time to the people. "It is our duty", they said, "to lay before the consciencies of French Catholics everywhere, the problem of the German prisoners of war." According to international law, repatriation depended upon a peace treaty; but the treaty with Germany had still not been signed although the war had ended three years before. Other nations, like the United States and Great Britain, had already effected their repatriation. Why was France waiting?

Archbishop Roncalli, worked very hard, with the full and continued approval of the Pope, to see that the situation did not degenerate into an injustice. In making a distinction between the German people and the Government of the Third Reich, he adhered to similar convictions which he had upheld previously in Turkey.

Needless to say Catholic France responded to the appeal which, as is now generally admitted, proved to be an important factor in the strengthening of European unity. Now that there exists a sense of brotherhood among European nations this episode in the Roncalli story will be looked back upon with especial interest.

It was from its ancient and traditional sense of humanity that France was able to find within herself the example, the principle, the basic standard, she needed; and she did this under the guidance of the men who represent and personify the tradition, the civilization and the humanity of France, just as had happened three years previously, when the same Cardinals and Archbishops published their fundamental declaration for the reconstruction of the country, with its 'five condemnations' of those social trends which had led to the war.

While the deputies at the Constituent Assembly were working out the details of the fundamental laws of the new State, the assembly of Cardinals and Archbishops agreed upon the following condemnations: (i) of working class conditions, "that is to say, of the state of uncertainty, of economic dependence and often of poverty which deprives numerous workers of any really human existence"; (ii) of the over importance being placed upon money, "so that the demand for profit and returns comes before a just concern for the needs of the workers"; (iii) of degenerate firms, "which instead of serving the community, are becoming a means of exploitation for personal interests and ends"; (iv) emphasizing class divisions between people, "united by essential common interests and who ought to come to an understanding for the common good"; (v) of materialism "which has sacrificed all human rights to the excesses of a soul-less rivalry and a thirst for money".

In the text they also express the hope that the workers will have gradual access to the possession of property; to the participation in the organization of his work, of the firm by which he is employed, and of society; the realization of a workers' organization through trade unions, management committees and mixed commissions.

The history of those years has brought it home to everyone just how apt were the solutions which the French Bishops proposed, not only for purely spiritual, but for economic and political problems.

It is possible now to realize also the clearsightedness and forethought of the Bishops' proposals. Of course, as was only too natural there were objections from people who thought themselves more enlightened, more modern and more progressive. Armchair revolutionaries are always prepared to let others be as rash as they please provided the result makes enough noise, is decently kaleidoscopic – and far enough away: a maxim which might be worth adding to the comfort offered by La Rochefoucauld when he reminds us that everyone has strength enough to bear the troubles of others.

Thus among the rest of the idle chatter at the intellectual tea-parties, they did not neglect to pass judgement on the *prêtres-ouvriers* (worker-priests). Indeed they did not stop short at talking about them; *Le Vieux Colombier* decided to give the subject a gala evening, crowded with South American diplomats. The cinema, too, did not want to be left out. But what nobody in fact knew was that for more than fifty years there had been priests in France who had had to earn a living by manual work as opticians, electricians or watchmakers, all on account of the laws passed by those who "simply cannot bear" to think of a lathe-operator who gets home at night and then says Mass before going down to the bistro to sup off coffee and a croisson. In just the same way, nobody remembered that the priests of the "Prado" had been a workers' mission for over a century, while the experiments proposed by the Abbé Godin in 1944 necessarily needed all the corrections and modifications that are an integral part of all experiments.

It will take a long time before such a priestly mission of this kind is running smoothly. It means that we must find a way of establishing human contact with those who are our brothers but who are not themselves aware of it. Even we are sometimes inclined to forget it.

That the working classes in France are largely atheist is a fact (30 per cent are not baptized); but the priests are in a ratio of one to eight hundred persons, that is, more than in Spain (1:830) or in Italy (1:1030).

It should be observed that the French clergy often come from upper middle class or noble families, which makes it difficult for the workers to feel close to them.

The experiment of the worker-priests is one of the many which attempted to reach the outer fringes of society. The search still continues to find new and more efficient methods. The apostolic zeal of the *Mission de France* has already led many atheist workers, and communists, back to the brotherhood of Christ.

For his part, the Nuncio had in those same years completed a mission which he had undertaken both as a friend and a priest. It had to do with Edouard Herriot, a radical professor of great force and prestige.

Archbishop Roncalli accosted him suddenly. "Mr. President," he said, bitterly aware of the man's hard, unflinching gaze and the tell-tale signs that a hard life had left on the face before him, "we have nothing standing between us but our political opinions. Don't they seem to you rather unimportant?" Herriot agreed, for he was a generous-hearted man, and from that time forward, the two met more and more frequently and a friendship grew up between them. But no-one ever knew anything about it until Herriot died as a Catholic in February 1957. This event aroused the old Radical element in France and even Daladier was not above exaggerating with his "plot against the Republic". Before he died, Edouard Herriot had two interviews with Cardinal Gerlier, and in front of his wife, he asked to be allowed to die a Catholic.

The truth is that it fell to the Nuncio to bow once before the representatives of progressive ideas. It was on an evening in January 1953 in the great hall of the Élysée Palace. The Pope had created Archbishop Roncalli a Cardinal and, according to tradition, the red biretta was placed on his head by the French chief of State. President Auriol, seeing the Nuncio kneeling before him, felt greatly moved. "He wasn't kneeling before me, an unbeliever, but before the Pope whom I was, for that moment, representing. But what struck me more than anything that evening was a sign of his pure goodness. He asked me, as a great favour, to invite the mayor of his native village and three or four Italian peasants to the Élysée Palace. All of them were moved to tears and wept throughout the ceremony. Can a Socialist remain indifferent to the tears of the workers?"

VENICE AND ROME

THE announcement, in November 1952, of his elevation
to the Sacred College had saddened the Nuncio. He had
received another message from the Vatican charging him
with the duty of informing Archbishop Feltin of Paris that
he, too, was to be created a Cardinal in the following January. He rung him up immediately to announce his impending visit. His friendly voice, however, could not disguise
his sorrow. Archbishop Feltin did not wait, therefore, to
be visited, but went straight to the Nuncio's residence. He
found Archbishop Roncalli reading his breviary in a
manner quite unbefitting a Cardinal of the Church.

"I'm going to end my days swathed in red tape," he
said. He shrugged his shoulders in silent comment. He
was, after all, a Bergamese and beneath his coat-of-arms
stood the motto *Oboedientia et Pax*.

"And just think," he added, "I should have been quite
content to be an ordinary pastor somewhere near Bergamo."

But when the next Vatican dispatch reached him, his

whole face lighted up. The Pope had decided to send him to Venice, as Patriarch.

It was going to be the ideal ending to his life: to be a shepherd of Christians. The thought reminded him of the shepherds who worked in the Imagna Valley. Also surely there had been another aged Bergamese who had become Patriarch of Venice? His practised scholar's mind sent him to check this. He found the book, and turned up the passage. Yes, he was right; but the other man had been five years older than he when appointed, yet had worked so hard that it would take at least five or six volumes to describe all that he had achieved.

Later, as he was leaving Paris amid the applause, the fanfares, the flag-waving and the bouquets, he felt sad again. The Patriarchate, he kept repeating to himself, was something too big for him. So many parishes, such a large number of souls, and such a glorious history.

When he arrived in Venice, he warned them: "Don't expect to find a diplomat in me, or a V.I.P. I'm only a parish priest and I want to remain so." In fact, according to a young, newly ordained priest, he bore himself "as a father, not as a police officer". Even as Patriarch, he kept up his habit of going round, continually visiting, seeing with his own eyes, asking questions and, above all, listening to all kinds of people.

On one occasion, when he was staying in Venice, President Auriol saw Roncalli coming into the foyer of his hotel. Finding people near him either kneeling or bowing, the President hesitated slightly, wondering what he should do. He need not have worried, for the next moment he found himself suddenly embraced, like a long-lost friend, by the Patriarch. They went together to the Patriarch's palace, where Cardinal Roncalli showed him Pius X's room, preserved exactly as it had been when the saint dwelt there, but now a museum. It was as humble as the room of a village priest.

"He was the child of poor parents, just as I am. And people like us don't need very much." There was a moment's silence, and then Auriol, feeling obliged to say something, commented that he was astonished to find no formalities there, everybody coming and going and able to talk quite freely to the Cardinal Patriarch. And indeed anybody could come in and speak freely with him.

Another visitor was Cardinal Wyszyński, who had been permitted to leave Poland in order to visit the Vatican. The Patriarch went to meet him at the station and took him on the Grand Canal.

When the Archbishop of Paris, Cardinal Feltin came to Venice on St. Mark's Day, 1955, Cardinal Roncalli showed him round the famous Cathedral. Later they heard Solemn Vespers together and his guest was forced to admit his admiration of all he had experienced in St. Mark's. Outside in the square a band was playing and the Patriarch asked them to play the Marseillaise for Feltin.

It was Cardinal Roncalli who decided that the Cathedral should be used for the Stravinsky concerts during the International Music Festival. He was also the first Patriarch for more than fifty years to visit the *Biennale di Venezia* (the art exhibition held every other year), as he thought that abstract art, which was so praised and fêted that year, at least had the advantage of not offending either morals or dogma. Also he had seen much modern painting in the Paris art galleries, even liking some of it.

In Paris he had got to know the work of Bernanos, Mallarmé, and even Rimbaud. This last was a poet who might have become a saint in the desert like De Foucauld, since he had the right temperament for it.

Whenever possible he still travelled about as a Papal Legate. He went to Lourdes by jet-plane – his tenth flight – to open the underground Basilica. He visited Fatima, Compostella and even Beirut. Sometimes he led diocesan pilgrimages. He visited Western Germany privately by car and expressed astonishemnt at that nation's post-war rebirth.

He was always happy, however, to have the opportunity of visiting Bergamo and walking in the surrounding countryside. At Sotto il Monte, near his brother's farm, he enjoyed the peace of the old house of his ancestor, Maitino Roncalli. In his simple native village he was content, undisturbed, close to nature and to the people, to his own origin. This was the expanse of country where his forefathers had worked. Here his father had toiled, here his brothers and nephews were still laboring. Like them, and the people with whom he stopped to speak in the local dialect, he seemed to be made of that soil.

On the death of Pope Pius XII it was known in Sotto il Monte that Cardinal Roncalli would be going to the Vatican to assist in the election. The parish priest had given an explanation of the proceedings at the end of Mass. During the following days the villagers sat expectantly by their radios waiting for the decision. At last it came, spoken in a Latin which even they could understand. *Annuntio vobis gaudium magnum: habemus Papam,* "I have joyful news for you", and then the name, *Angelum Josephum Roncalli.*

In the kitchen of the Roncallis' house, where their friends often gathered to listen to the wireless on the dark winter evenings, they all stared at one another, confused, happy, even terrified. Saverio and Giuseppe couldn't get up from their chairs, but remained where they were, weeping silently. Then suddenly the women and the young men present began to shout "Viva il Papa – Long live the Pope", as the darkness outside was suddenly shattered by the light of countless bonfires dotted all over the surrounding countryside.

The excitement did not cease, but all through the night remained at the same high pitch. Reporters and photographers kept on arriving, the headlamps of their noisy cars blazing. They all wanted to know the same things. The names of his parents, where he was born, what he had done and where. The questions went on and on. And what they could not discover they imagined, as their reports later proved!

And so the Patriarch of Venice, like Saint Pius X, one of his predecessors, emerged from the Conclave as Pope. On Sunday, October 26, 1958, seventeen days after the death of Pius XII, the fifty-one cardinals – only Cardinal Mindszenty and Cardinal Stepinac had had to remain behind, while Archbishop Mooney of Detroit had died suddenly in Rome shortly before the Conclave – had withdrawn behind the locked doors. On Tuesday, October 28, following the twelfth ballot, the eagerly awaited white smoke rose up into the evening sky, and almost immediately following this, Cardinal Canali (as first Cardinal Deacon), speaking from the balcony of St. Peter's to the hundreds of thousands in the square below and to an expectant radio audience of millions, announced both the civil and the pontifical name of the new Vicar of Christ.

At the railway station in Venice, when leaving for the Conclave, Cardinal Roncalli had said: "Everybody is wishing me luck; my only hope is that I can return here again in two weeks." But as in the case of Cardinal Sarto, the return half of his ticket remained unused.

How the votes were divided from ballot to ballot, how many Cardinal Roncalli gained each time, and how many were finally cast for him remains a secret entrusted to the electors alone. Forbidden to bind themselves to vote in any particular way before the election, they may not, on pain of severest ecclesiastical chastisement reveal its secrets. In the same way they are forbidden to have any contact with the outside world during the Conclave itself. Therefore all the suggestions made in the Press concerning the motives of the electors who, it was alleged, had formed themselves into groups in order to determine the out-come, were unfounded. As the Pope later declared, the reporters had shown great talent for guessing, but the Cardinals an even greater one for remaining silent.

All we do know is that the final number of votes had to

be at least one more than a two-thirds majority, as provided for by canon law. In this case the final number was thirty-five. When this required majority was reached the Cardinal Deacon, in the name of the Sacred College, asked the one chosen whether he accepted the election. Cardinal Roncalli answered: "Your words fill me with fear and trembling, but as a I recognize in the election of my excellent brothers, the Cardinals of the Holy Roman Church, the sign of God's will, I accept the choice they have made. I bow my head before the chalice of bitterness and my back under the yoke of the Cross. Let it be as we sang on the Feast of Christ the King (the day the Conclave began): "The Lord is our lawgiver, the Lord is our King: He will save us."

Few had supposed that His Holiness would take the name John, which had been used more often than any other. Indeed, the title John XXIII had previously been used, but by an anti-pope. The depths of his personality, however, and his own particular piety, determined his choice of a name. The Pope himself has explained to us that it was dear to him, being the name of his father, of his native parish church, and of countless Catholic churches throughout the world, including, above all, his own Cathedral, the Archbasilica of St. John Lateran. Saint Mark, the patron of Venice, also bore the name John.

In addition it calls to mind those two great New Testament figures, John the Baptist and the Beloved Disciple. A final reason, in which we recognize both the historian and the man eager to cope with difficult problems, was his wish, as the rightful John XXIII, to see the anti-Pope, Baldassare Cosse, elected in Bologna by the "Pisa Party", finally excluded from all lists of legitimate popes.

In his coat of arms His Holiness has chosen to commemorate both his origins in Sotto il Monte and his connections with Bergamo and Venice. The tower is adopted from the Roncalli crest painted on the house in Sotto il Monte, while the two fleurs-de-lys are the emblem of the martyr, Alexander, diocesan patron of Bergamo. The winged lion, carrying an open book on the pages of which are written *Pax tibi, Marce, Evangelista meus,* symbolizes Venice.

The solemn coronation, on the balcony of St. Peter's, took place after an exhausting four-hour ceremony in the basilica itself. This was attended by representatives of Church and State throughout the whole world, while radio and television allowed millions of people to participate.

Characteristic is the address given by His Holiness during the coronation Mass. "Everyone has been busy assigning to me that role which, in his personal opinion, is

most important. There are, in fact, those who expect the Pontiff to be a statesman, a diplomat, a scholar, a social organizer; one, in fact, whose mind is open to all forms of progress in modern life, without any exception. None of those, however, who have made these suggestions, have succeeded in entertaining a concept of the supreme pontificate which conforms in every respect to the true ideal. It is the task of a new Pope to make that splendid image of the Good Shepherd a living reality. He is the door of the sheepfold.

"Into this fold of Jesus Christ no one can enter except under the guidance of the Sovereign Pontiff; and men can securely reach salvation only when they are united with him, since the Roman Pontiff is the Vicar of Christ and represents His person on earth . . . .

"We have at heart, in a very special manner, our task as shepherd of the entire flock. All other human qualities – learning, diplomatic insight, organizing ability – can succeed in embellishing the reign of a Pontiff but they cannot in any way serve as a substitute for this. The central point, however, is the zeal of a good shepherd, ready for every sacred undertaking, no matter how daring, straightforward, constant, even unto the supreme sacrifice. If necessary he engages in combat with the wolf in order to defend his sheep."

10

THE FIRST BROADCAST

On Wednesday, October 30, 1958, His Holiness, Pope John XXIII, spoke to the world for the first time in a short Latin address over the radio. The following is the text of his message.

Following the death of Our predecessor, Pius XII, of universal memory, so faithful and worthy a minister of the Catholic Church, this onerous burden of the Pontificate has been laid upon Us by the mysterious will of Divine Providence: in this hour, therefore, when anxiety weighs upon Us and oppresses Our heart, let Us, before all else, raise up heartfelt prayers to God that He, in His infinite goodness, may strengthen Our weakness, illumine Our mind, and fortify Our will.

Let Us most warmly embrace Our beloved brethren of the Sacred College of Cardinals, whose resplendent gifts and spiritual virtues We well know; and let Us turn

especially to those among them who it grieves Us to know are so far from Us, and whose suffering and distress so deeply move Us.

We desire also to express Our fatherly loving-kindness to the venerable brotherhood of bishops, who labor throughout the world to tend the Lord's vine. Nor may We neglect to mention the priests, for they are the dispensers of God's mysteries: especially, We would mention the Missionaries, who, as harbingers of the Holy Word, spare no sacrifice to spread the Gospel-truth in distant lands; the monks and nuns who join in the work of the Church with an enlightened zeal; those lay workers who fight under the guidance of the bishops in the un-armed forces of Catholic Action; and all those others who help the bishops and priests of the Church in whatsoever way they can. We bless them all, We bless them, each and everyone, with an overflowing heart.

Next, We pray to God for all Our children in Christ, but especially for the poor and the suffering: We pray that He may abundantly grant to all of them the help they need, and His heavenly comfort. Of all Our children, those particularly dear to Our fatherly heart are the flocks of the Venetian lands, whose shepherd We once were, and of the diocese of Bergamo, where We were born; and if We are now far from them, We are, none the less, ever near them in the love of Jesus Christ, and shall be for evermore. We trust, moreover, that their prayers, joined unto Ours, may rise up to God and be visited with His heavenly grace.

Our thought goes out in a special way to the bishops, priests, nuns, and all the faithful, living in those countries where the Catholic religion enjoys little or no freedom, where the sacrosanct rights of the Church are recklessly trampled underfoot, where the lawful pastors are exiled or confined or kept from the free performance of their duties as ministers. We wish them to know that We share their pain, their grief and their distress; and We beseech the Lord, giver of all things good, that He may put an end, once and for all, to this inhuman persecution, which not only undermines the peace and prosperity of these peoples, but is also in flagrant contrast with modern civilization and the long-undisputed rights of man. May God send His light into the minds of those countries' leaders; may He forgive the persecutors; and may He speedily grant to all those who do enjoy their lawful freedom, better and happier days.

This for the Western Church: but with no less strong a fatherly love do We embrace the Eastern Church. We open Our arms and Our heart in like manner to all those who are divided from this Apostolic See where Peter

himself lives in his Successors "even unto the end of the world" (Matt. 28: 20), fulfilling the order given him by Christ to bind and to loose everything on this earth (cf. Matt. 16: 19), and to feed the lambs of the Lord (cf. John 21: 15, 17). We eagerly desire that they should return into the house of Our Common Father, and We therefore repeat the words of the Divine Redeemer: "Holy Father, keep through Thine own name those whom Thou hast given me, that they may be one, as we are" (John 17:11). And in this way "there shall be one fold and one shepherd" (John 10:16). We therefore entreat them, that they may all come, with a whole-hearted and a loving will; and that their return to the flock may be accomplished at the very earliest with the inspiration and the help of Grace. They shall not enter into a strange house, but into their own; that same house as was once made glorious by the renowned doctrine of their forefathers, and made precious by their virtue.

And may We make Our appeal to the rulers of all nations who hold in their hands the destiny, the well-being, and the hopes of their peoples. Why will they not settle, once and for all, the world's strife and discord? Why are the resources of the human brain and the wealth of the nations bent most often to the invention and manufacture of weapons, pernicious instruments of death and destruction, rather than to the greater welfare of all sorts and conditions of men, particularly of the less fortunate among us? We know, it is true, that in the carrying out of such a laudable aim, and in the settling of disputes, we shall meet with grave and perplexing difficulties; but these must be victoriously overcome, even though the victory require great effort, for this is the highest task of all, and one which is closely bound up with the prosperity of the whole human race. Come, act courageously and confidently in this great work, bathed in the light from on high and with the help of God. Turn your gaze upon the people entrusted to your charge, and give ear unto their voice. What do they ask of you? What do they entreat? They do not ask for those monstrous engines of war, the discoveries of our age which bring with them fratricidal slaughter and wholesale massacre: They cry for peace, that peace by whose virtue the human family may freely live, flourish and prosper. They want a justice that will settle once and for all, fairly and equitably, the rights and duties of the different classes. And lastly, they want peace and amity, for only from this can any real prosperity arise. Provided that such a peace be based in the lawful rights of all men, and provided that it be nourished with brotherly love, it will become a fertile field where the arts and culture may spring and flower, where the energies

of all men shall be joined in an active virtue, and where the wealth of men and of nations may increase. Let us remember what great men of the past have thought about this. St. Augustine (*The City of God,* xix, 13) says that peace is "an ordered harmony among men". St. Thomas Aquinas (ii–ii, 29, i–i) says that "it is tranquility within order". Cicero (*Philippics* ii, 44) says that "peace has a sweet name, but her meaning lies much deeper. There is, though, a vast difference between peace and slavery. True peace is peace in freedom."

It is fitting to ponder and consider with lively attention what the angels sang above the cradle of the Holy Child: "Glory to God in the Highest, and on earth peace to men of Goodwill" (Luke 2:14). Peace cannot light upon nations but through the people; peace cannot light upon people but through their souls: for outward peace cannot exist unless it be a reflection of inward peace, and unless it be ruled and guided by this inward peace without which everything totters and threatens to fall. Faith in God, therefore, is the only thing that can nourish it, strengthen it, and firmly establish it. Let this truth be remembered by all those who reject the name of God, who revile His holy laws, and who stop at nothing to expunge all sense of piety from the human breast.

In this grave hour We remind you of the words and

promises of the Divine Redeemer: "Peace I leave with you, my Peace I give unto you" (John 14:4), and as a token and a pledge of this true and universal peace, as well as of all the other gifts of Heaven, We give with Our most fervent and intense love the Apostolic Blessing on Rome and on the world.

11
EPILOGUE

WHEN he was in charge of the student's hostel at Bergamo, Don Roncalli had a large mirror fixed on the wall at the turn of the stairs, and in order to make sure that the boys would remember to make themselves tidy before going out, he added a notice which read:

Nosce te ipsum (Know thyself).

★

When he was called to Rome by Benedict XV in 1921, he was at once called Monsignor. So, when he went home to Sotto il Monte for his holiday, he celebrated a special Mass. He seemed a real bishop to the peasants and afterwards an old woman asked his mother for an explanation.

"What do you want me to say? These are things that the priests fix up between themselves."

★

In August, 1952 Archbishop Roncalli's brothers came to visit him in the Nuncio's residence. He put his huge diplomatic car at their disposal and they remained out all day. One evening, he asked Giuseppe if he would like to remain in Paris.

"Just give me the opportunity!" came the unmistakable reply.

On the morning after their arrival, the four were late in coming downstairs. The Nuncio, therefore, went up and found them all looking very exasperated, their ties in their hands. They didn't know how to tie them.

"Well, how did you manage yesterday?" he asked.

"The women at home tied them for us."

"Never mind, go around without. After all, I never wear them."

★

Dumaine, Master of Ceremonies at the Élysée Palace, asked the Nuncio personally whether it ever annoyed him when the ladies who were presented to him wore very low-cut dresses.

"I don't look at them," he replied, "and what's more, neither do the other men, for when these women arrive, the men all turn round to see how the Nuncio's taking it."

★

Archbishop Roncalli and Albert Schuman often went together to antiquarian bookshops. They even arranged to exchange some volumes.

One day, the Nuncio found a fourteenth-century illuminated codex. It was certainly Italian, and as he turned over the pages he discovered something more. It was Bergamese, from the ancient convent of Santa Grata.

He asked the price but the bookseller quoted a figure far beyond his means. However, two friends got to know about this and gave it to him as a present. He spent a very long time studying it, and then gave it to the library in Bergamo.

★

They asked him how it was that he always got on so well with everybody.

"There's nothing wrong with my liver, there's nothing wrong with my nerves: so I like meeting people."

★

At a reception in Paris, they were talking about Lourdes. One of the guests came up to the Nuncio and began to pester him with questions about whether he really believed in this or that cure.

Finally Archbishop Roncalli stopped him. "Do you

really believe that illness is a subject to be discussed in the drawing room?" he asked.

★

"I shall speak very simply to my Venetians about our good Saint Mark," said Cardinal Roncalli, explaining his program to the Venetian clergy, who had come to pay their respects after his appointment as Patriarch.

"Then you will speak to them in dialect?" hazarded one.

"Well, I might. I think I could master it within two months."

★

The Cardinal met Father Spiazzi in the Vatican during the days preceding the Conclave, and he reminded the priest that he was expecting to see him in Venice for a conference in November.

"Of course I shall come," replied Father Spiazzi, looking at Cardinal Roncalli over his glasses, "but you never know what may happen here in Rome between now and then."

★

Cardinal Roncalli used to wear a rather shiny and thread-bare cassock. He explained, "The stuff is excellent, though. From before the first war. It belonged to my Bishop, Monsignor Radini-Tedeschi."

Later, when they drew lots for their "cells" during the Conclave, he drew the room of the General of the Noble Guard. Other members of the Conclave pointed out an omen on his door, a nameplate bearing the one word "Commandant".

★

On the evening of his election the new Pope returned to his appartments. The servants were still busy setting everything in order. He settled down in the most likely corner away from the confusion of people and furniture and started to read his breviary. His secretary, Monsignor Capovilla, asked him whether he should telegraph the news to his relatives.

"Yes, please do!" he replied, "and since I'm behind with my office, I'll say Vespers in the meantime."

★

On one of the days following his move to the Vatican, His Holiness heard someone hammering loudly in the room above. He went upstairs to investigate. He found his secretary's apartment being put in order. He knocked at the door.

"Come in", said the workman, who nevertheless remained bent over his work. The Pope entered and

103

asked him what he was doing. The man turned around and seeing the Holy Father knelt down, but could only stammer:

"Your Holiness, Your Holiness."

Those working in the next room asked him to whom he was talking.

"The Holy Father", came the reply.

"Oh yes?"

"Yes truly, by Our Lady."

Whereupon the Pope walked to the door connecting both rooms and said:

"Your friend speaks the truth. I came to see what you were doing. Perhaps you would explain one or two things to me."

★

On his return from his having taken possession, as Bishop of Rome, of his Cathedral church, the Archbasilica of St. John Lateran, Mother and Head of all the Churches, the crowds greeted the Pope with enthusiastic cheering. He responded again and again with his blessing, and many times was on the point of doffing his hat as had been his custom in Venice. When, however, they entered the Piazza della Chiesa Nuova, he finally removed his hat with a flourish and said, "I am now saluting the graves of St. Philip Neri and the historian Cesare Baronius."

★

The first time he visited Castel Gandolfo, he appeared on the balcony to the crowds cheering in the street below. Among them was a farmer who was known to be a communist. He was soon recognized and was asked by a friend what he was doing there. "He is a worker's son, he knows what work means, and I'm clapping for the poor people's Pope."

★

When paying a visit to the College of the *Propaganda Fide,* he asked the Rector not to waken those students who had dropped asleep during the reading of the first hours. "Very well, Holy Father," he replied, "but if they expect permission to sleep during my lectures, they are going to be bitterly disappointed." The Pope laughed.

★

The Pope has regular working habits, certainly, but, like a true Italian he never maintains an absolutely rigid system. Before his election he would often get up at two in the morning and sit working at his desk until five or so, and then return to rest for a few hours.

105

Today, in the Vatican, he does the same, and recently the priests who help him became rather worried and told him that they, too, were very willing to work at night.

"But I do this", he replied, "especially so that I can work undisturbed."

★

His Holiness is fond of saying: "Always respect the dignity of those you are with and, above all, the freedom of every human being. God himself does so!"

NOTES

[1] Tenant farming in Italy is a very ancient institution, although now it is falling into disuse through the continual disputes to which it gives rise; another, perhaps more important, factor in the decay of the system is that the landlords are still able to live in the town but can easily drive out to their property every morning and work it with machines. Because of this the tenant farmers of the past have largely been replaced by independent farmers.

[2] The text of the baptismal certificate is as follows:
Anno Milles. Octing. Octag. Primo (1881)
Die vigesima quinta (25) 9bris
Ego Fr. Rebuzzini Par. huj. Eccl. S. Ioan. Bapt. Sub
Monti baptizavi infantem hodie natum ex leg.
Conj. Ioannes Bapt. Roncalli, et Mazzola Marianna
e Brusico huj. Par.: cui impositum est nomen
Angelus Joseph. Patrinus fuit Xaverius Roncalli
fil. Ioannis Bapt. huj. Par. In quor. fid. Sac.
Franciscus Rebuzzini Parochus.

In the year eighteen hundred and eighty-one, the twenty-fifth day of November, I, F. Rebuzzini, pastor of this parish of St. John the Baptist, Sotto il Monte, baptized the child born this day to the lawfully wedded Giovanni Battista Roncalli of this parish and Marianna Mazzola of Brusico his wife, who was given the name of Angelo Giuseppe. The godfather was Saverio Roncalli, son of Giovanni Battista of this parish. Certified by Francesco Rebuzzini, Parish Priest.

[3] Angelo Giuseppe Roncalli, son of Giovanni Battista and Marianna Mazzola, has three brothers and one sister, although until a few years ago, all ten were still living. He is the eldest; then came Saverio, married, with no children; Alfredo, still a bachelor; Giuseppe, a widower with five sons and five daughters; and Assunta Marchesi, a widow with four sons. In 1957, the youngest brother, Giovanni, died, leaving eight children, one of whom, Battista Roncalli, is a thirty-year-old curate at Fusignano in the Diocese of Faenza near Bologna. One of Battista Roncalli's sisters is a nun in Rome, and one of his nieces, Sister Maria Anna, has been a nun for nearly ten years and now works at a Mission centre in Asmara, Eritrea.

Assunta Roncalli, the Pope's sister, married a Milanese workman called Marchesi and went to Sesto San Giovanni, a suburb of Milan, where she is now living with her daughter and son-in-law, who themselves have three children.

A more distant relative, Giovanni Colombo, is one of many Italian bricklayers working in France. He lives at Villers-Franques near Rheims, and when in March 1958, Cardinal Roncalli was visiting Lourdes as Papal Legate, this bricklayer went to see him there. There are apparently several families named Roncalli living in France, and they all come from around Bergamo.

[4] Monsignor Camillo Guindani was one of that succession of Bergamese bishops which is historically so very important. He is best known for his work in preparing the way for his great successor, Radini-Tedeschi, who will be spoken of at greater length later.

At a very difficult time, when hundreds of Italian bishops were hindered in the exercise of their duties by the Government, or even forcibly removed and imprisoned for their loyalty to the Pope, Guindani (see F. Vistalli, *Monsignor Guindani nei Suoi Tempi,* Bergamo, 1943) was strong enough to be able to make Bergamo a free region where the people of "the real Italy", as they then called it, pitted themselves victoriously against "the official Italy" of the Government which had installed itself behind the bayonets of the occupying forces, who entered without any declaration of war.

Italy, during the second half of the nineteenth century, was a land not so very different from those countries where today the Church is called the "Church of Silence".

[5] In 1877 Count Stanislao Medolago-Albani became president of the diocesan committee that stood at the head of the 366 parish councils forming the center of the whole Catholic movement, and Niccolò Rezzara was at once made vice-president. Together with this committee, whose function was one of general organization, there came into being, in the same year, the Diocesan Union of Catholic Social Institutions. Towards 1884, it became clear that the latter was superceding the former. Certain people began to think that, with the notable development of the Catholic associations and workmen's mutual benefit societies, there was no longer any real reason for the existence of the parish councils, so several of them were disbanded while others were just permitted to disintegrate. Rezzara was very worried about this changing state of affairs. "Experience has shown", he wrote, "that no Catholic association can completely replace the parish councils" (N. Rezzara, *Il Movimento Cattolico nella Diocesi di Bergamo. Appunti e Statistiche,* Bergamo, 1897, p. 4). The reference is important from a historical point of view because it shows how Bergamo foresaw problems

and changes, in this field as well, which did not became evident to the rest of Italy for another twenty years.

Count Medolago-Albani was one of the several generous-spirited Italian noblemen who set their keen sense of social problems to work during the years at the end of the last century and the beginning of this. He was the most illustrious of that succession of noblemen whose last representative is Count Giuseppe Dalla Torre di Sanguinetto, head of the Vatican newspaper *L'Osservatore Romano* since 1919, and the first leader and legislator of the well-known Italian Catholic Action.

Niccolò Rezzara, who was born in Vicenza in the north of Italy, was an exceptional secondary school teacher, a provocative journalist (founder of the *Campanone* and manager of *L'Eco di Bergamo*), a keen organizer and trades unionist. Among other things he successfully led the 1909 strike which gained for the workers the right to belong to a union (see G. Belotti, "Don Angelo Roncalli e Bergamo Cattolica", in *L'Osservatore Romano*, November 6, 1958).

[6] The Bergamese, Flaminio Cerasoli, who was a canon in Rome during the eighteenth century, established a foundation there, which awards scholarships to Bergamese students wishing to go to the Roman Pontifical Seminary. It was by this means that Angelo Roncalli

came to be one of those chosen to study in the Eternal City.

[7] The Radini-Tedeschis are an ancient and noble family of Swiss origin. Carlo (1829–1908) and his son Giacomo, who finally became bishop, threw themselves zealously into the activities of the great nineteenth-century Catholic revival.

The Crispi Law was passed by the Italian Parliament in 1890. It was an unjust law designed to get possession of property belonging to workers' religious associations, whose members had no resources apart from this property, which they themselves administered. In order to counteract this law, Count Carlo Radini-Tedeschi founded advice and assistance bureaus in the most important towns, trying to save whatever could be saved. His speeches on the judicial and economic aspects of the subject, which he made at the National Catholic Congresses in Lodi (1890), Pavia (1894), and Milan (1897), are very important. As a consequence, the Charities Section of the National Standing Committee of the Conference Movement found in him an energetic chairman.

[8] See *L'Osservatore Romano,* January 24 and 26, 1905.

[9] A. Roncalli, *In memoria di Monsignore Giacomo M. Radini-Tedeschi, vescovo di Bergamo* (Bergamo, 1916), p. 230.

[10] His penetrating monograph called *Chiesa e Stato in ordine ai concordati* (Milan, 1887), is an abridged version of the thesis he wrote on Canon Law for his degree.

He was born in Piacenza in 1857, took a degree in Theology at the Gregorian University in Rome, and then another in Genoa, where his mother came from. He worked in the offices of the Vatican Secretary of State from 1890 to 1896, receiving his training from Rampolla. He was made Papal Ablegate to Vienna and to Paris, but the appointments were honorary rather than political – the secular equivalent would be the head of an extra-ordinary diplomatic mission – and both times he took with him an extremely learned priest, Achille Ratti of the Ambrosian Library in Milan, who was later to become Pope Pius XI.

Radini-Tedeschi was a fine orator, and he made a point of turning up at all the Catholic conferences in that period. His speeches in 1883, 1892, 1894, 1896 and the Holy Year 1900, were famous.

To give some idea of how busy he was before a bishopric was conferred upon him, suffice it to say that by the end of 1900, he had made 1300 speeches in different parts of Italy.

[11] Cardinal Nina, Vatican Secretary of State, was said to have died of a broken heart, as a consequence of the

tension between the Vatican and Brussels. This was the result of the Belgian hierarchy receiving different instructions, via the Auditor Sanctissimus (this post no longer exists, but the holder's function was to transmit the Pope's personal wishes to the appropriate quarters), from those which Nina had given to the Nuncio.

[12] It was perhaps the first time in the history of the Vatican that a Pope had been told that diplomatic trickery was something repugnant to a Christian conscience.

[13] *Pataria* is a word whose original meaning is equivalent to the Latin word *plebs* taken in its narrow and contemptuous sense. Later the word was applied to the lower classes generally. Finally, in the eleventh century, the word came to be referred to the popular religious and social movement against the privileges and the misuse of power exercised by the clergy.

[14] Ten days after Rome was taken, the Central Committee of Catholic Youth decided to start a movement designed to unite all the forces of Catholicism on the lines of similar Belgian and German movements. Since this movement was organizing an annual national rally in the form of conferences it was called the Conference Movement.

It should further be noted that Catholic Youth dates back to 1867, the year when the forces of the State made two unsuccessful attempts to enter Papal Rome; one by monarchist volunteers commanded by one of the King's officers, and the other by republican volunteers commanded by Garibaldi.

[15] Radini-Tedeschi's elevation to the See of Bergamo should be considered in connection with the crisis in the Conference Movement brought about by pressure from and attacks by the *Giovanni* and the *Murriani* groups. An overt conflict manifested itself between the two factions in the stormy Nineteenth Catholic Congress (Bologna, October 10–13, 1903), though there had been previous signs that all was not well at the *Graves de communi* on January 18, 1901, and in the Secretary of State's instructions of February 27, 1902. These had led to several other signs of malaise: Count Grosoli's being substituted for Count Paganuzzi as president of the Conference Movement in October 1902; the controversy between Toniolo and Murri; the open letter written by A. Lazzarini and G. B. Bertini on August 29, 1903, suggesting a course of trades union and political action on the part of Catholics over and above anything for which the bishops would take responsibility. This was condemned on the following October 7 by Cardinal Merry del Val as "irreverent and rebellious", just three days before the Bologna Congress was due to open, and it showed how far people still

were from "a movement independent of ecclesiastical authority". This was not to come into being till many years later, thanks to the Popular Party. See F. Magri, *L'Azione Cattolica in Italia* (Milan, 1953), vol. i, pp. 193–4.

On July 2 of the following year, again at Bologna, only the Standing Committee of the Conference Movement met: next to the new chairman, Grosoli, sat the vice-chairmann, Monsignor Radini-Tedeschi. But the meeting was far from orderly, and when St. Pius X, then Pope, received Radini-Tedeschi afterwards he expressed his deep disappointment. The famous breech then widened: only the documents in the archives can throw any light upon it, although there is a publication just out which includes actual extracts from the Belgian Foreign Office records. See R. Aubert, "Documents relatifs au mouvement catholique italien" in *Rivista di storia della Chiesa in Italia,* vol. x (1958), p. 202 et seq. It is already known that the Grosoli circular dated July 15, replying to the letter of July 6 that he had received from Cardinal Merry del Val, had been written by Meda and Radini-Tedeschi. On July 18, like a bolt from the blue, *L'Osservatore Romano* published their refusal to recognize this same circular; which brought about the resignation of the whole Board of the Conference Movement.

The crisis lasted until the end of July, and led to the

Movement being wound up, except for the famous Second Section, concerned with social and economic action, run by Count Medolago-Albani, another Bergamese.

[16] A. Roncalli, op. cit., p. 134.

[17] It was very different when King Victor Emanuel III made an official visit to Bergamo. But this was not until 1913, and *L'Osservatore Romano* (September 24 and 25, 1913) gave prominence to the reports of the visit, thus indicating to the public the Vatican's verdict on the event.

[18] A. Roncalli, op. cit., p. 90 et seq.

[19] A. Roncalli, op. cit., p. 90 et seq.

[20] Before entering the Conclave from which he was to emerge as Pope, Cardinal Roncalli wanted to visit the tomb of Baronius in the "Chiesa Nuova". While he was there he confided to his companion how his admiration for the sixteenth-century Cardinal had increased over the years; in fact he had adopted the motto from Baronius' coat of arms: *Oboedientia et Pax*. He inquired also about the bibliography on Baronius and expressed great admiration for the work of Calenzio.

His book was printed in Monza in 1908, the year following the centenary.

[21] The discovery gave birth to his excellent book – *Atti*

della Visita Apostolica di San Carlo Borromeo a Bergamo (1575), in the "Fontes Ambrosiani" series, edited by the Biblioteca Ambrosiana (pub. Olsky, Florence). The story of how the original idea was conceived and how it came to be realized is to be found in the introduction, p. 29 et seq.

[22] The *Atti* are still in the course of publication, exactly half a century after the work's conception.

A copy of the first volume is now kept in the Vatican library; it was the gift of the author to his adviser, and it bears this autograph note:

"First copy, humbly offered with my hands to His Holiness, Pius XI, with feelings of deep gratitude more than ever alive after so many years, with the particular expression of devotion and love and the wish that His Holiness himself may grant his blessing for the fulfilment of this work, et ultra.

Castel Gandolfo	Angelo Gius. Roncalli
September 25, 1936.	Archbishop of Mesembria,
	ap. deleg. to Turkey and
	Greece.

Here we have two Popes discussing the past together, completely unaware of the future that awaits them. In the introduction to his book, Archbishop Roncalli says, "I well remember my first shy and uncertain meeting with

Ratti. In the far right-hand corner of the old room chosen for our consultation, the librarian welcomed me with gracious, dignified friendliness, and I can still see the expression that spread over his face as he listened to an idea which appealed to him as both worthwhile and interesting, but on which he reserved definite judgement until after he had seen the documentary material.

Only a few days after that first meeting, Ratti had already looked through the whole of the voluminous collection of correspondence in the archives of the Palace. Two volumes, vi and vii, contained all the minutes and orders of the day regarding the inspections of city and diocese; they seemed, therefore, to be the obvious web into which would have to be woven all the other documents, which he had sorted out on his work-table ready for photographic reproduction. He was kind enough to say that he personally would see to the reproduction of all the sheets in these two volumes, using a process which was still more or less in the experimental stage, but which turned out very well indeed. Not content with that, he took over the responsibility of collating all the separate photographs and of arranging them with his own hands in such a way that it would not be necessary to refer to the original manuscripts again, for these had to be returned to their place in the archives. Not only did he praise but his words were full of approval and encouragement. Monsignor Ratti taught me a lesson I have never forgotten: that the curator of a library was not just someone who looked after books but one who used his knowledge for the furtherance of sound study."

Radini-Tedeschi, like the great organizer he was, had the idea of co-ordinating it and placing it under the direction of his young secretary. "He made the project known throughout the diocese and entrusted the seminary with the job of carrying it out. From among the teachers he selected a commission, warmly encouraged them in public and gave them financial help – the first they had ever received. But as always happens, it began with a commission and finished up with only one person doing the work."

[23] This might well serve as warning to all who set about writing the history of Italian Catholic Action: instead of drawing their subject matter from foreign sources, they would do better to examine Italian ones. Many are of the opinion that Catholic Action grew out of the secret societies, Christian Friendships as they were called, organized by the Jesuit Diessbach, in the second half of the eighteenth century. What they do not realize, among other things, is that an enormous society, not entirely secret, existed even among those laymen who had

been to Jesuit colleges at least as far back as the seventeenth century. There were also those little groups and circles which produced members of the Zelante Party in Rome and in the Papal States during the following century.

So one can see how, apart from the much more remote origins of the Catholic charitable institutions (hospitals, loan-offices, etc.), the cultural conventions which took an active part in political life date, not from the end of the nineteenth century, but from the late seventeenth or early eighteenth.

[24] A. Roncalli, La 'Misericordia Maggiore' di Bergamo e le altre istituzioni di beneficenza fatte dalla Congregazione di Carità (Bergamo, 1912).

The expert way in which the material is handled shows how clear the conception of the thousand-year-old origins of the charitable institutions and their perennial energy must have been in the mind of the author, who continually explains ancient documents by bringing them into the light of modern experience. (There is no lack of subtle illusions to nineteenth century events. For example, speaking about the Napoleonic invasion and the Jacobite rebellions, he refers to certain democrats, "among whom were to be found many noblemen who had become democrats for the occasion".)

That the historical research didn't stop short at the

archives, but ranged also over the artistic records of the Middle Ages, is obvious right from the frontispiece, a reproduction of a fifteenth century fresco showing several Bergamese folk making a collection for the citizens' institution.

From certain hints to be found in the text, for example, see p. 66, it would appear that his work on St. Charles Borromeo's visitation was in progress at the same time.

[25] A. Roncalli, *In Memoria,* pp. 77–8.

[26] Idem, op. cit., p. 79.

[27] Idem, op. cit., p. 76.

[28] Idem, op. cit., p. 80.

[29] Idem, op. cit., p. 99.

[30] *La Civiltà Cattolica,* November 25, 1904, pp. 544–5.

[31] Political reorganization among the Italian States after Spain had established herself in the peninsula (Lombardy in the north, the Papal States in the center, and in the south the Kingdom of Naples) had been on the program of the French Court since 1753. They wanted a federation of national and independent states under the leadership of the Pope, who was already sovereign of the Federation of Papal States. Paris' policy changed with the expeditions of Napoleon, which won Italy from Spain and brought her under French subjection. The fall of Napoleon and the Congress of Vienna led to a strained and clumsy reconsti-

tution of the peninsula which now passed under Austrian rule.

Into the general picture of Europe in 1848, which was revolutionary but widely Catholic, there enters the first war of the Italian League (Piedmont, Tuscany, the Papal States, and the Kingdom of the Two Sicilies) against Austria who, apart from a political influence over Italy, held territorial securities in the possession of the Kingdom of Lombardy-Venice. The very varied and changing ideological movement which led to that war was largely characterized by neo-Guelfism, which took up the French idea of 1753 and proposed a federation of National States with the Pope at its head.

The war was lost in 1849 and soon new tendencies came to the fore. These wanted the old classes and the old states abolished, and replaced by a single classless state. Therefore the war began again, this time contrary to the hopes of Paris, who still wanted a federation led by the Pope. It led to a succession *coups d'état* against the various Italian sovereigns, not excluding the Pope. For a start, he was deprived of all his so-called "Legations" – all, that is, except Latium – but even this single survivor was invaded and finally conquered in 1870 after an unsuccessful attempt in 1867.

[32] At the Congress of Milan on April 5, 1905, Count

Medolago-Albani spoke about the last remaining section –
the Second Section – of the disbanded Conference Movement, and gave the following statistics:

2432 economic social institutions in all parts of Italy,
including the following:

774 Mutual aid societies
21 People's Bureaus
107 Workers' or Consumers' unions
170 Professional and Workers' Leagues
33 Rural unions
43 Agricultural unions
29 Collective rent societies
69 Banks
835 Agricultural aid groups
40 Working men's aid groups
154 Co-operative animal husbandry centers
187 Christian Democrat Propaganda Associations
(see Magri, op. cit., p. 223).

[33] A. Roncalli, *In Memoria,* p. 99.

[34] F. Magri, op. cit., p. 96.

[35] *La Civiltà Cattolica,* November 26, 1910, p. 613.

On the occasion, the Bergamese Rezzara spoke on the
professional organizations, for which he proposed a
system of single trade unions and mixed unions. The
proposal excited the antagonism of those who already

sympathized with what we now term left-wing tendencies, but which then went under the name of "class resistance" (pp. 618–19). The unusual form of the attacks aroused, in its turn, the displeasure of the president. F. Crispolti, who warned them that "congresses are useful, but not indispensable". (With the Bertini Order of the Day the definition "democratic initiative" was born. p. 614.)

[36] F. Magri, op. cit., p. 291.

[37] *La Civiltà Cattolica,* February 8, 1913, pp. 476–86.

In its full report, the magazine points out the exceptional interest aroused by Dalla Torre's first speech, which he made in Venice in February of that year. The subject is referred to again on p. 495.

[38] G. Belotti, "Don Angelo Roncalli e Bergamo Cattolica", in *L'Osservatore Romano,* November 6, 1958.

[39] Also A. Roncalli (op. cit., p. 102) states that the Bishop, "In his usual honest and forthright way, gave a clear picture of what the state of affairs really was, and the real part that everyone had played in it. He said that the information had been neither admissible nor entirely objective."

[40] "Sometimes, particularly in the closing years of his life, he was troubled by uncertainty and doubts as to whether he still merited the entire confidence of the

Pope. This was the greatest trial of his virtue, and although this is a delicate subject to be spoken of today, it would be too great an offence against truth and against the real merits of Monsignor Radini to say nothing about it at all." (A. Roncalli, op. cit., p. 184). But even in 1911, the Bishop of Bergamo had had to clear himself, in the Pope's eyes at least, of the charge of not being realistic enough in the face of the facts, of seeing things in too a rosy light. On November 26, he wrote thus: "A 'too rosy view of things', Holy Father, has earned me the public accusation of being autocratic, uncompromising, unbending and dictatorial; it has made the Public Prosecutor name me a Papist who still upholds the dominion of Church over State – and this on the solemn opening of the Session of the Brescia Court of Appeal; it has made the Chief Justice harshly upbraid me and threaten to deprive me of my temporal rights" (A. Roncalli, op. cit., p. 185).

[42] Also to be considered alongside the official reports are the formal words of address spoken by Roncalli when Pius XI granted him public audience in October 1925. He was conducting a second Bulgarian pilgrimage to see the Pope. (*Cronistoria dell'Anno Santo MCMXXV*, Vatican City, 1928, pp. 352–3 and p. 509.)

[43] These statistics are taken from official reports made in 1930, to be found under "Bulgaria" in the *Enciclopedia*

Cattolica compiled by the Pontifical Institute for Eastern Studies in Rome, For information on the Slav Byzantine Rite, see also *La statistica con cenni storici della gerarchia e di rito orientale,* edited by the Congregation for the Eastern Church, Vatican City, 1932, pp. 104–5, where the increase in educational institutions and the increase in Catholic Action are also recorded.

[44] The non-recognition was preferred by a number of countries. Nowadays, however, the Diplomatic Corps accredited to the Vatican is made up of ambassadors and ministers from some fifty countries, including Mohammedan and other non-Catholic countries (China, India, Indonesia, Iran, Pakistan, etc.). The Vatican reciprocates by sending Papal Nuncios.

[45] *L'Osservatore Romano,* January 18, 1933.

[46] *L'Osservatore Romano,* January 19.

[47] *L'Osservatore Romano,* November 11, 1926.

[48] Bulgaria was the only country to allocate in its National Budget large sums for Russian and Armenian refugees.

[49] He was also transferred to the titular See of Mesembria.

[50] Historically speaking, it was Pope Leo XIII who denied the validity of Anglican ordinations. The Synod of the Russian Orthodox Church received a request for recognition in 1903, but they too refused. In 1938, the

Greek Orthodox Church recognized Anglican ordinations, after having considered the matter since 1931.

[51] In 1927, a group of Greek Orthodox laymen began
to publish the magazine *Zoe* (Life), which, as might be
supposed by the title, tried to infuse a little life into Greek
religious institutions. The hospitals, workhouses and
charitable institutions generally are extremely successful,
though this is also due the judicial settlement of relations
between Church and State. The *Aktines* group began in
1938; it corresponds in a way to the Catholic intellectuals'
movements.

[52] When John XXIII was elected, the newspaper
Kathimerini published an article called "The good work
of the new Pope: Pope John XXIII's work in Greece
during the occupation".

[53] Gratitude has been expressed by the Chief Rabbi of
Israel: he sent Cardinal Roncalli a telegram congratulating
him on his election as Pope.

[54] The Armenian Catholic primateship in Constantinople dates back to 1461. In 1759, the Vatican set up a
Vicariate Apostolic in Constantinople for the Armenian
Catholics, which was the starting point for the various
attempts at ecclesiastical reorganization, with a See
sometimes in Constantinople and sometimes in Lebanon.
The last re-arrangement made in 1925, followed the

massacres within the Turkish Empire between 1915 and 1919, and after the Russian invasion of Caucasian Armenia. It concerned those Armenians who had emigrated to Greece. There is a Pro-Cathedral in Athens; with four parishes spread over the whole Kingdom of Greece. The Vatican made similar arrangements for the large Lebanese group of Armenian Catholics in 1928, and the Rumanian group in 1930.

[55] *Statistica,* p. 112.

[56] The head of the Latin Catholics in Turkey is, if we wish to be precise, the Latin Patriarch of Constantinople. But this is merely an honorary title, which during the years about which we are writing had been bestowed upon Monsignor Rossi, ex-archbishop of Udine, who lived in Rome and Pompeii. He confessed that he knew nothing of Constantinople save what he had gleaned from a collection of oil paintings presented to him by some monks.

[57] Baron von Papen, a Catholic, was at that time German Ambassador at Ankara. Perhaps he had been entrusted with a mission, not unlike General von Bronsard's in 1914, to bring Turkey in on Germany's side. In any case he was clever enough to make certain that Turkey did not side *against* the Third Reich, although the Allies were doing all they could to persuade her to do so. When the

outcome of the war became obvious, von Papen offered the Vatican representative a number of papers. This was in order to get the Pope to intercede with the allies and try to persuade them not to make the German people pay too heavily for all the Third Reich had done. He found Cardinal Roncalli's co-operation in the matter very keen and friendly: and one part their negotiations came to light during the Nuremberg trials.

[58] On December 10, 1914, until the break-up of the Empire, he was in continual and very friendly relations with the Grand Vizier. He was also a warm and much heeded friend of Generalissimo Enver Pasha. (A. Lazzarini, *Breve biografia del Cardinale Angelo Dolci,* Rome, 1941, pp. 79, 83, et seq.)

[59] Many of the ideas contained in the New Year radio message which De Gaulle broadcast a few hours afterwards to the French people, had already been expressed in the Nuncio's speech of good wishes – that France would cease to be a battlefield and that 1945 would bring steady, if slow, progress.

[60] A deeply religious sense is inherent in the family of De Gaulle, where tradition plays a very important part just as it does throughout the really old French nobility. De Gaulle did not ask for any action to be taken against the Catholic hierarchy as such, only that purely personal

measures be taken against those bishops who, in the public's opinion, had compromised themselves.

[61] *L'Osservatore Romano,* November 7, 1945, announced that Pius XII had accepted the resignation of the Bishops of Arras and of Mende who had been replaced three days before by Monsignor Perrin and Monsignor Rousseau; the Sees of Blois and Aix which thus became vacant were filled the same day by Monsignor Robin and the famous De Provenchères.

[62] There are some areas, like Vandea, where the private school children amount to 70 per cent. The Western regions usually have from 40–60 per cent, the southern regions from 22–50 per cent.

By means of various laws, (for example, the Barange Law, the Billières Law), those in power are trying to establish a monopoly of State schools by withdrawing the subsidy to private schools. Only in the regions of the Moselle and the Upper and Lower Rhine, lands returned to France by the Treaty of Versailles, do private schools receive any subsidy. Ever since 1871, Germany had scrupulously respected the Falloux Law which came into force at the time of Napoleon III. France also continued to do so after 1918, and the situation there has not changed.

[63] The insinuation was made by Hervé in March, 1946, during the fierce controversy he had with Mauriac in

Humanité and *Figaro*. In August of that year there was a Constituent Assembly at which the communists repeated the charge that the clergy had acted "according to their own illusions" during the occupation and the period of the Vichy Government. The M. R. P. group therewith withdrew from the debate.

[64] The Bishops of Nice, Clermont-Ferrand, and Tarbes-Lourdes, and the Archbishop of Carthage, all fought hard to help those families which had had no wages coming in for so long.

The Episcopate had already intervened in this matter with the collective pastoral of Christmas 1947, inviting a settlement and pointing out that the workers had gained no advantage from the interminable strikes. In the previous November, Cardinal Suhard, Archbishop of Paris, had made an appeal to all the workers, Catholics and non-Catholics alike, explaining just how the right to strike should be used.

In the spring of 1950, the bishops took the part of the workers, trying to procure them a wage increase. The Bishop of St. Brieux made it known that hardly 25 per cent of the laboring population received an adequate wage, while the Bishop of Limoges warned employers to "bear in mind that the workers are the life-blood of production".

LIST OF IMPORTANT DATES

1881, November 25	Born in Sotto il Monte (Bergamo).
1904, August 10	Ordained in Rome in the church of Santa Maria in Monte Santo, on the Piazza del Popolo.
1905, January 31	Returned to Bergamo as secretary to the new Bishop, Monsignor Giacomo Radini-Tedeschi. Holds post as seminary professor.
1915–8	Military service as sergeant in the Medical Corps. Later as Lieutenant Chaplain in Bergamo.
1921, March 12	Appointed by Pope Benedict XV to be President of the Italian branch of the Society of the Propagation of the Faith. Then member of the new General High Council of this papal world mission.
1921, May 7	Nominated Domestic Prelate.
1925, March 3	Nominated titular Bishop of Areopolis, with the title of Archbishop.
1925, March 19	Consecrated in the church of San Carlo on the Corso, and appointed Apostolic Visitor to Bulgaria.

1931, October 16	Appointed first Apostolic Delegate to Bulgaria.
1934, November 30	Given the title of Archbishop of Mesembria.
1935, January 12	Took up post in Istanbul as Vicar Apostolic and Apostolic Delegate to Turkey, and Apostolic Delegate to Greece.
1944, December 22	Appointed by Pope Pius XII as Apostolic Nuncio to France.
1953, January 12	Created a Cardinal by Pope Pius XII, with the titular church of S. Prisca.
1953, January 15	Appointed Patriarch of Venice.
1958, October 28	Elected Pope.

INDEX

Agazzi, G. B., see Battistel
Aix-en-Provence 131
Aktines group 128
Alexander, Martyr 90
Alps, The 1, 2
Amalfi 55
Ambrose, St. 4
Ambrosian Library 30, 44, 45, 47
American students 16
Anatolia 55, 62
Anglican ordinations 127
Ankara 55, 63, 129
Anthony, St. 8
Areopolis 50
Armenians 60–1, 127, 128–9
Arras, Bishop of 131
Asia 60
Asmara 108
Assisi 53
Ataturk, Kemal Pasha 61–5
Athens 55, 57 et seq., 60
Auditor sanctissimus 114

Augustine, St. 97
Auriol, Vincent 75, 84
Austria 123

Balkan States, The 50; *Entente* 57; Wars 49, 59
Barange Law 131
Baronius, Cardinal 29 et seq., 105, 117
Basil of Tirnovo 49
Battistel 10
Beirut 85
Belgium 27, 45, 114, 116
Belotti, Giuseppe 40
Benedict XV, Pope 44, 45, 99
Bergamo 1 et seq., 11–15, 19, 21, 26, 30, 32–3, 37, 40–1, 43, 65, 75, 82–3, 86, 90, 93, 99, 101, 109, 110, 115
Bernanos, Georges 85
Bernardine of Siena 8
Bertini, G. B. 115

135

Bey, Vassiv 63

Beyoglu Cathedral 59

Bidault, Georges 67, 69, 73

Biennale, Venice 85

Billières Law 131

Blois 131

Bologna 108, 115, 116

Boris III, King of Bulgaria 53, 57

Borromeo, St. Charles 31, 118, 122

Bosporus 62, 66

Brembo, River 65

Brescia 2, 126

Bronsard, General von 129–30

Brusico 8, 10

Bucharest 63

Bulgaria 48–54, 57, 59, 126, 127

Bulgarian Orthodox Church 48, 49

Bussilkoff, Eugene 51

Byzantine Rite Catholics 50, 52, 58, 59, 127

Calenzio 117

Cameroni, Agostino 34

Campanone, Il 111

Canali, Cardinal 87

Canossa, Ottavio 36

Capovilla, Monsignor 103

Carthage, Archbishop of 132

Carvico 11

Castel Gandolfo 105

Catholic Action 32, 33, 47, 60, 72, 93, 111, 120, 127

Celana 11

Central Committee of Catholic Youth 114

Ceppetelli, Giuseppe 19

Cerasoli, Flaminio 111

Chaldean Catholics 61

China 61, 127

"Church of Silence" 110

Cicero 97

Civiltà Cattolica, La 122, 125

Clermont-Ferrand, Bishop of 132

Colombo, Giovanni 109

Compostella 85

Conference Movement 25, 33, 112, 114, 115, 116, 124

Congregation for the Eastern Church 50, 59, 127

Congregation for the Propagation of the Faith 48

Congress, Catholic 25

Constantinople 49, 61, 63, 128, 129; also see Istanbul

Co-operative Animal Husbandry Centers 15
Co-operative Dairy 15
Crispi Law 112
Crispolti, Filippo 125
Croix, La 72

Dalla Torre di Sanguinetto, Giuseppe 40, 111, 125
Dandelion 59
Declaration of Principles 39
De Gaulle, Charles 67–9, 130
De Provenchères 131
Detroit 87
De Vecchi 8
Diessbach, Nikolaus 120
Diocesan Union of Catholic Social Institutions 110
Dolci, Angelo 63, 64
D'Ondes-Reggio 36
Donizetti, Signor 10, 11
Dumaine, Jacques 73, 100

Ecclesiastical Union for Social Studies 15
Eco di Bergamo, L' 111
Ecumenical Congress 56
Edinburgh 56
Enciclopedia Cattolica 127

England, the English 56, 76
Entente, Little 57
Eritrea 108
Etruscans 2, 5

Faenza 108
Falloux Law 131
Fatima 85
Feltin, Cardinal 82, 84–5
Fermo Proposito, Encyclical 37
Ferrari, Andrea 30
Ferrata, Domenico 73
Figaro, Le 132
Foligno 5
France, the French 45, 61, 69 et seq., 109, 122, 131
Fusignano 108

Galatia 64, 66
Garibaldi 115
Garigliano, River 24
Gasparri, Pietro 63
Genoa 55, 113
Gerlier, Pierre 81
Germany, Germans 45, 76, 85, 114, 131
Giovanna of Savoy, Princess 53
Giovanni group 115
Godin, Abbé Henri 79

Graves de communi 115

Greece, Greeks 49, 55–7, 59, 60, 128, 129

Greek Orthodox Church 48–9, 55–8, 60, 128

Gregorian University 113

Gregory VII, Pope 24

Grosoli, Count 115, 116

Guindani, Camillo 13, 109

Herriot, Édouard 80–1

Hervé, Gustave 69, 131

Holland 45

Holy Land, The 20

Holy Year 1900: 18, 113; 1925: 45, 47

Humanité, L' 69, 132

Imagna Valley 5, 83

India 127

Indonesia 127

Innocent III, Pope 49

Iran 127

Istanbul 55, 57, 59, 60–1, 64

Italian League, War of 123

Italy 1, 3, 13 et seq., 22 et seq.; 35, 45, 61, 109, 110, 113, 123

Jacobites 61

Jews, The 58, 128

John, St. 90

John the Baptist, St. 90

John XXIII, Pope 89; List of Important Dates 133; First Broadcast 92

Kathimerini 128

Ketteler, Wilhelm Emanuel von 21

Kiosseivanoff 57

Klagenfurt 2

Kurteff, Kyrill 51–2

Lambeth Conference 56

Latin Rite Schools 56

Laudes Bergomi 65

Lazzarini, Andrea 130; Antonio 115

League of Nations 57

Lebanon 128, 129

Leo XIII, Pope 18, 21, 22

Limoges, Bishop of 132

Locarno, Treaty of 55

Lodi 112

Lombardy 1, 66, 122; –Brigade 42; –Venice 123

Lourdes 20, 85, 101, 109

Lozé, Maurice 67
Lucca 3

Macassoli 8
Macedonia 48, 49 et seq., 52,
    57
Maitino, see Roncalli, Martino
Malabar 61
Malgara 59
Mallarmé, Stéphane 85
Mangili 8
Marchesi, Assunta, see Roncalli
Marchetti–Selvaggiani, Arch-
    bishop 50
Marelli, Monsignor 44
Margherita, Queen Mother
    26
Maria Louise of Bulgaria, Prin-
    cess 53
Mark, St. 89
Mark's Cathedral, St. 85, 102
Mastai–Ferretti, Giovanni, see
    Pius IX
Mauriac, François 131
Mazzola, Marianna, see Ron-
    calli
Meda, Filippo 36, 116
Medolago-Albani, Stanislao 15,
    110–11, 117, 124

Mende, Bishop of 131
Merry del Val, Cardinal 115–
    16
Mesembria 127
Milan 1, 4, 30, 43, 108, 112;
    Congress of 123
Mindszenty, Cardinal 87
Misericordia Maggiore, La 32,
    121
Missionary Exhibition 46–8
Mission de France 80
Montorio 5
Monza 117
Mooney, Cardinal 87
Mosè del Brolo 65
Moselle 131
M.R.P. 71, 132
Murriani group 115
Mutual Aid Societies 15, 124

Naples, Kingdom of 122
Napoleon 121–2; — III 131
National Catholic Congress 39,
    112
Neri, St. Philip 105
Neuilly 48, 49
Nicaea, Council of 54
Nice, Bishop of 132
Nicopolis 51, 52

Nineteenth Catholic Congress 115
Nina, Cardinal 113, 114
Nogara 2
Nolis, Pietro 11
Non expedit 34, 36–7
Nullo, Francesco 4
Nuremberg 130

Oboedientia et Pax 82, 117
O.R.I.M. 48
Osservatore Romano, L' 41, 111, 112, 116, 117, 125, 127, 131
Ottoman Empire 49, 50, 55

Paganuzzi, G. B., Count 115
Pakistan 127
Palermo 20
Palica, Archbishop 50
Pangalti 66
Papacy 24
Papal States, The 24, 121–3
Papen, Baron von 129
Paris 35, 66, 67, 74, 83, 101, 113, 122
Pataria 24, 114
Pavia 112
Pecci, Gioacchino, see Leo XIII
Perrin, Monsignor 131

Petrik 57
Philippopolis 51
Piacenza 113
Piccinelli, Giuseppe 34
Piedmont 1, 123
Pinay, Antoine 74
Pisa 55, 90
Pius VI, Pope 25
Pius IX, Pope 21, 25, 30
Pius X, Pope St. 19 et seq., 27, 87, 116
Pius XI, Pope 30–1, 45, 47, 48, 51, 53, 54, 113, 118, 120, 126
Pius XII, Pope 92
Po, River 24
Poland 4
Pomarancio 6
Pontida 11
Pontifical Institute for Eastern Studies 127
Pontifical Society for the Propagation of the Faith 45
Popular Party 116
Prado 79
Prisoners of War 75

Quai d'Orsay 69, 73
Quirinal 14

Radini-Tedeschi, Carlo 20, 112

Radini-Tedeschi, Giacomo 19 et seq., 22, 26, 28, 30–3, 37, 40, 41, 44, 102, 109, 112, 113, 115, 116, 120, 126

Rampolla 113

Ranica 26-7, 40

Ratti, Dr. Achille, see Pius XI

Ravenna 20

Rebuzzini, Francesco 9, 107–8

Rezzara, Niccolò 15, 40, 41, 44, 110, 124

Rheims 109

Rhine 131

Rimbaud, Arthur 85

Riquet, Michel 71–2

Risorgimento 35

Robin, Louis 131

Romanoff, Eugene 51

Roman Seminary, The 45, 111

Rome 6, 14, 16 et seq., 22, 24, 29 et seq., 36, 41, 42, 49, 51, 53, 87, 113, 114, 115, 121

Roncaglia di Cepino 5

Roncalli, Alfredo 108

Roncalli, Angelo – born 8; childhood 9–12; training 13–18; ordained 19; priest in Bergamo 21–41; soldier 42–4; Rome 45–8; Bulgaria 50–4; Turkey and Greece 55–66; France 67–82; Venice 83–6; Pope 87–98; see also chapter 11 and Notes.

Roncalli, Assunta 12, 108

Roncalli, Battista 8, 108

Roncalli, Bernardo 8

Roncalli, Cristoforo 6

Roncalli, Giovanni 108

Roncalli, Giovanni Battista 8, 107–8

Roncalli, Giuseppe 10, 86, 99, 108

Roncalli, Sister Maria Anna 108

Roncalli, Marianna 8, 9, 99, 107–8

Roncalli, Martino (Maitino) 5, 7 et seq., 86

Roncalli, Saverio 86, 107–8

Roncalli-Frosio 5

Roncalli-Parolini 5

Roncalli-Peretti 5

Roncalli coat of arms 8, 90

Rossi, Anastasio 129

Rousseau, Monsignor 131

Rovigo 5
Rumania 49, 129
Russia 127
Russian Orthodox Church 127

St. Brieux, Bishop of 132
Saint Peter's, Rome 6, 19, 51, 88
San Pellegrino 1
Sarto, Giuseppe, see Pius X, St.
Scotti 8
Schuman, Albert 101
Schumann, Maurice 74
Sentierone 1
Serio, River 65
Sesto San Giovanni 108
Sicily, Kingdom of 123
Sofia 49–54, 57
Sofia-Philippopolis, Apos. Vicar of 52
Somasca 11
Sotto il Monte 5, 7 et seq., 19, 42, 86, 90, 99, 107–8
Spain 122
Spiazza, Raimondo 102
Stepinac, Cardinal 87
Suhard, Cardinal 132
Swiss Code of Law 62

Syrian Catholics 61
Tacci, Giovanni 50, 59
Tarbes-Lourdes, Bishop of 132
Theodora, Empress 61
Third Reich 76, 129
Thomas Aquinas, St. 97
Thrace 49 et seq., 52
Toniolo, Giuseppe 39, 115
Trent, Council of 31
Turkey 55, 57, 60–5, 76, 129
Tuscany 2, 3, 5, 123
Tyrol 2

Union of Electors 41
United States of America 76
Uskudar 66

Vandea 131
Vatican 16, 20, 22, 23, 25, 31, 36, 41, 50, 52, 53, 56, 59, 60, 62, 63, 66, 67, 82, 86, 114, 128, 129
Venice 2, 55, 83–5, 88, 90, 93, 102, 125
Versailles, Treaty of 131
Vicenza 111
Vichy 69
Victor Emanuel III, King 117

INDEX

Vienna 113; Congress of 122
Vieux Colombier, Le 79
Vistalli, Francesco 145
Vix 2

Worker-priests 79 et seq.

World War I 41 et seq., 59; II
58, 62
Wyszyński, Cardinal 84

Zelante Party 121
Zoe 128

LIST OF ILLUSTRATIONS

1. Pope John XXIII. (Frontispiece)
2. The simple farmhouse where Angelo Roncalli was born.
3. The toil-warn face of Giovanni Roncalli, the Pope's father.
4. Even today his brother Saverio looks every morning to see whether the hens have laid well.
5. The newly ordained priest "Don Angelo".
6. Near Pope St. Pius X in the Sistine Chapel. (The priest holding the Missal is Don Roncalli.)
7. With a striking moustache: as sergeant during the First World War.
8. In the papal diplomatic service as Apostolic Delegate to Turkey and Greece.
9. Archbishop Roncalli, delivering to General de Gaulle, on behalf of the diplomatic corps, the New Year's Day message of greetings.
10. The socialist Herriot is obviously surprised to find a pastor in the Papal Nuncio.
11. During an official audience the President of the French Republic presents him with the red biretta in the name of the Pope.
12. "What next?" the newly elected Cardinal appears to be asking himself. The way will lead him to Venice.

LIST OF ILLUSTRATIONS

13. On the Grand Canal. The Venetian sun shines brightly . . .

14. . . . likewise the face of this gondolier, winner of the historical Regatta against Pisa and Amalfi.

15. At Palermo Airport the Patriarch of Venice meets dignitaries of the Eastern Church.

16. Cardinal Roncalli paying a visit to the famous Venice *Biennale*.

17. The departure for the Conclave means farewell to Venice.

18. The Cardinals paying their respects to the newly elected Pope.

19. Cardinal Tien, now sick and homeless, experiences the warm-hearted concern of the Holy Father.

20. His Holiness is always pleased to meet visiting diplomats. Here he is seen speaking with West German Foreign Minister, von Brentano.

21. Cardinal Spellman pays homage to the newly elected Pope.

22. The Holy Father being borne through St. Peter's on the Sedia Gestatoria.

23 and 24. Inside St. Peter's during the coronation mass which was attended by Cardinals and Bishops representing nearly every country in the world.

25. "Oremus". Clad in full papal vestments, His Holiness prepares to give the blessing "Urbi et orbi".

2

3

4

6

7

8

9

11

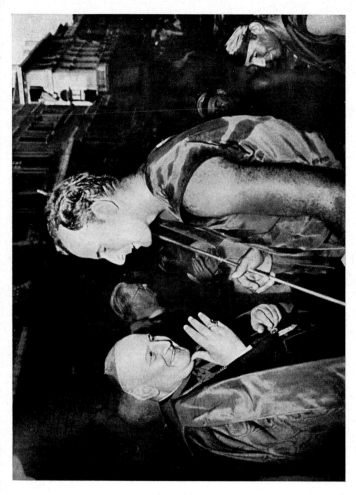

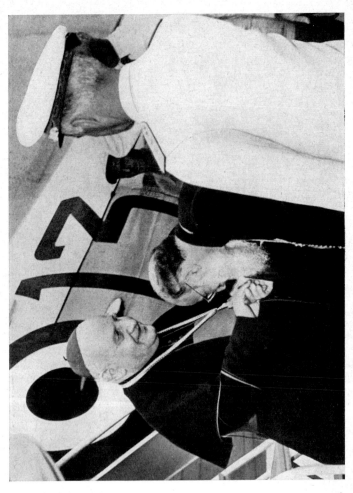

15

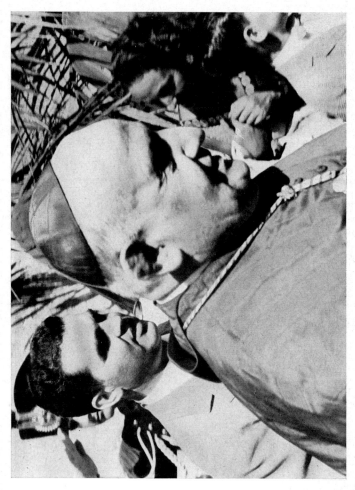

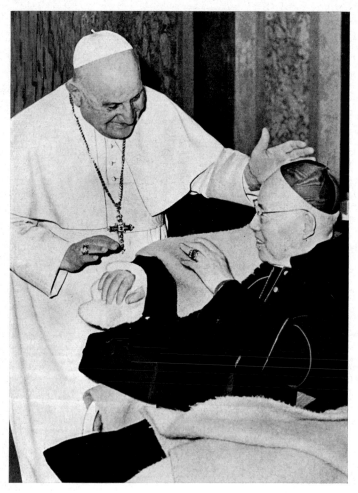

21

22

CHALLENGING RACISM IN THE ARTS:
CASE STUDIES OF CONTROVERSY AND CONFLICT

In this insightful and lucid analysis, framed by their contention that
'cultural production is one way in which society gives voice to racism,'
Carol Tator, Frances Henry, and Winston Matthis examine how six con-
troversial Canadian cultural events have given rise to a new 'radical' or
'critical' multiculturalism.

Mainstream culture has increasingly become the locus for challenge
by racial minorities. Beginning with the Royal Ontario Museum's *Into
the Heart of Africa* exhibition, and following through with discussions of
Show Boat, *Miss Saigon*, the exhibition of the Barnes collection at the Art
Gallery of Ontario, the Writing Thru Race Conference in Vancouver, and
the ill-fated attempts to acquire a licence for a Black/dance radio station
in Toronto, the authors examine manifestations of racism in Canada's
cultural production over the last decade. A 'radical' multiculturalism,
they argue, is difference as a politicized force, and arises whenever cultural imperialism is challenged.

CAROL TATOR is Course Director at the Department of Anthropology,
York University.
FRANCES HENRY is Professor of Anthropology, York University.
WINSTON MATTIS is a lawyer specializing in employment law.